ALSO BY SUSAN CERULEAN

Tracking Desire: A Journey after Swallow-tailed Kites

UnspOILed: Writers Speak for Florida's Coast
(edited with Janisse Ray and A. James Wohlpart)

Between Two Rivers: Stories from the Red Hills to the Gulf
(edited with Janisse Ray and Laura Newton)

The Wild Heart of Florida (edited with Jeff Ripple)

The Book of the Everglades (editor)

Florida Wildlife Viewing Guide (with Ann Morrow)

Guide to the Great Florida Birding Trail: East Section
(edited with Julie Brashears)

Coming to Pass

Coming to Pass

Florida's Coastal Islands in a Gulf of Change

SUSAN CERULEAN

PHOTOGRAPHS BY DAVID MOYNAHAN

The University of Georgia Press *Athens & London*

Bill Holm's poem "New Religion" is from Holm's collection *The Chain Letter of the Soul: New & Selected Poems* (Minneapolis: Milkweed Editions, 2009). Copyright © 2009 by Bill Holm. Reprinted with permission from Milkweed Editions. www.milkweed.org. Parts of chapter 2 originally appeared in *Flycatcher*; parts of chapter 12 appeared in *UnspOILed: Writers Speak for Florida's Coast*, edited by Susan Cerulean, Janisse Ray, and A. James Wohlpart (Tallahassee: Red Hill Writers Project/Heart of the Earth, 2010). "Saint Island Prayer" originally appeared in *The Gulf Stream: Poems of the Gulf Coast*, edited by Jeff Newberry and Brent House (Valdosta, Ga.: Snake Nation Press, 2013). The map on page 6 is by Lou Cross. The maps on pages 36, 50, and 222 are by Matthew Clark Smith.

© 2015 by the University of Georgia Press
Athens, Georgia 30602
www.ugapress.org
All rights reserved

Designed by Erin Kirk New
Set in Minion

Printed and bound by Thomson-Shore

Printed on 100% post-consumer recycled paper

The paper in this book meets the guidelines for permanence and durability of the Committee on Production Guidelines for Book Longevity of the Council on Library Resources.

Most University of Georgia Press titles are available from popular e-book vendors.

Printed in the United States of America
19 18 17 16 15 C 6 5 4 3 2

Library of Congress Cataloging-in-Publication Data

Cerulean, Susan.
   Coming to pass : Florida's coastal islands in a gulf of change / Susan Cerulean ; photographs by David Moynihan.
      pages   cm
      Includes bibliographical references.
   ISBN 978-0-8203-4765-3 (hardback)
   1. Islands—Florida—Apalachicola Bay. 2. Apalachicola Bay (Fla.)—Environmental conditions. 3. Island ecology—Florida—Apalachicola Bay. 4. Coastal ecology—Florida—Apalachicola Bay. I. Moynihan, David, photographer. II. Title.
   GB475.F56C47   2015
   577.5'20975991—dc23   2014037292

British Library Cataloging-in-Publication Data available

New Religion

This morning no sound but the loud
breathing of the sea. Suppose that under
all that salt water lived the god
that humans have spent ten thousand years
trawling the heavens for.
We caught the wrong metaphor.
Real space is wet and underneath,
the church of shark and whale and cod.
The noise of those vast lungs
exhaling: the plain chanting of monkfish choirs.
Heaven's not up but down, and hell
is to evaporate in air. Salvation,
to drown and breathe
forever with the sea.

BILL HOLM
The Chain Letter of the Soul: New & Selected Poems

CONTENTS

The Passing of a Palm Cathedral

CABBAGE TOP is a crescent of sand, thin as the smile of a three-day moon. Like every bit of Florida's coastline, it is sinking into the sea.

This floating cathedral of palm trees tethered to St. Vincent Island's furthest flank is a singular orienting feature in Apalachicola Bay. But when winter fogs zipper the horizons up tight, you can't see Cabbage Top at all. You lose even the cardinal directions until the sun burns back through.

Of all St. Vincent Island's wild geographies, Cabbage Top—labeled on older maps as Paradise Point—had seemed the most impossible to reach, on foot or by boat. I often thought about it as I explored other parts of the island, wondering what it might look like and how I might approach it. I imagined a deeply shaded hammock, refuge of red wolf and sambar deer.

My husband, Jeff, and I chose a clear February morning to run our skiff up the miles of the sound and explore the place for ourselves. We timed our trip to take advantage of a full moon–swollen tide and a predicted swing of the wind from west to south to east. The bitter air would run at our backs both coming and going, easing our travel along the sound.

We motored past things we knew: a favored resting place of white pelicans and the Pickalene Bar, where redfish run and wintering bald eagles squat among the oysters. We flew right by the mouth of Big Bayou, where Buddy Ward's sons still hold oyster leases and watch over the coming and going of each boat that ventures into that shallow bay.

"Give me a stab!" called Jeff.

I leaned over the boat's nose and sounded the water with a paddle.

"Still got two feet," I said. "I think we're going to be good."
I scrambled back to the stern, and we floated our unweighted bow right up to Cabbage Top's beach. I jumped ashore and looped a line around the trunks of two palms. To the east, a tidal creek defined the island's end. The western tip tailed off into a palm-flush strand overtopped by two slash pines tall enough to serve a single eagle. One pine was dead, its roots killed by salt.

Many of the palms were dying as well. If you only thought of the headless trees as beautiful pillars holding up the sky, if you had never heard their emerald fronds talking in the wind, then the lopped-off tops of the trees might not have saddened you. Maybe you would not even know what voices no longer were speaking— I mean the ceaseless clattering leaves of the palm, which translate the air's movement into a language louder and more specific than any words. You might have said that the empty chalice of a root ball, where a palm recently stitched to the land, was a baptismal font. You might have tipped your fingers into that round rain-water pool and tasted its wild-caught liquid on your tongue. You might have stroked the smooth concrete of one of the trunks and believed it fine and strong. You might have drummed your hands against it, and the tree would have responded to your touch with a hollow thrum, a tall percussive instrument standing in the sun. But if you laid your weight against it, both you and the tree would have fallen.

That day on Cabbage Top I understood with my eyes and in my bones what the scientific data so clearly show: the oceans are swelling. Florida, the last landscape on our continent to emerge from salt water, is sifting back into the sea. Our coast will never be the same as it is today, not even tomorrow. I looked around Cabbage Top, a point of land I had only just met, a crowded barge of dying green plants, a refugee from its own island. I knew its time was limited.

CABBAGE TOP sits on the trailing margin of northwest Florida. There, at the mouth of the Apalachicola River, four islands—Dog, the two St. Georges, and St. Vincent—stud a slim necklace of emergent sand that dangles into the Gulf of Mexico. To the west and the east, the peninsular spits of Alligator Point and Cape San Blas clasp the chain to the coast. Perhaps if you studied a map or a satellite photo, you wouldn't see the curve of a necklace but something more like a wishbone. Cape San Blas and the islands could be clavicles hugging their lagoons to the land, and Cape St. George, the bold breastbone, their point of fusion.

This stretch of Gulf Coast, like all the edges of our continent, has served humans so well that we believe its present configuration will always be under our feet. Nearly three-quarters of Florida's human population live or work in coastal areas. Even when hurricanes rearrange whole communities and roads fall into the sea, we cash in our insurance and rebuild. We think of these coasts as permanently constrained by legal definition or at least by an informal agreement cemented over generations of living by the water.

THROUGHOUT MY LIFE as a biologist and a writer, I have worked for several nonprofits and two state agencies searching for ways to protect Florida's natural lands and wildlife. I wrote about the endangered Florida panther and the splendid swallow-tailed kite, and how to create a backyard refuge for wildlife. I helped design a program to monitor Florida's nongame wildlife, and as data from those bird counts and mammal surveys accumulated, I began to understand the downward trend in numbers—and in numbers of kinds. Always, it seemed to me that my colleagues and I worked in a defensive stance, trying to shore up losses.

During all these years, the northern Gulf Coast has been my refuge. I wanted to learn its islands as if I'd always lived there, and as if unbroken generations of my people had before me. I wanted to learn the intricacies of bird migrations and how to feed myself

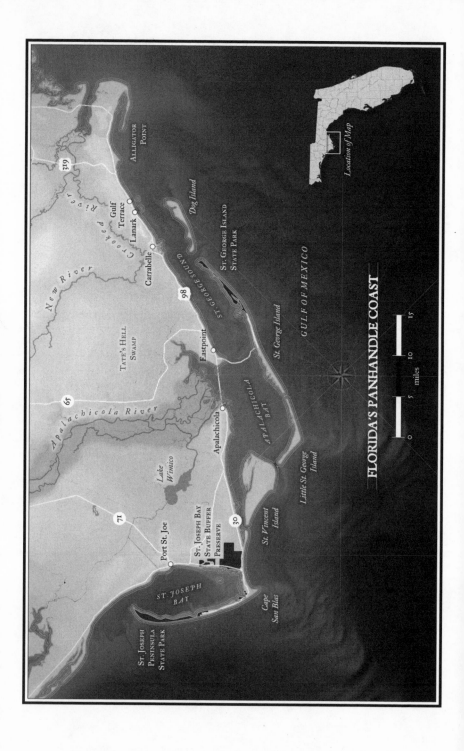

FLORIDA'S PANHANDLE COAST

and my family from the sea. As I camped, fished, and counted birds, I became curious about the age of the islands and how they had come to be.

But the world was already changing. I could see how storms and the rising sea were rolling over the black needle rush marshes where clapper rails slip and seaside sparrows sing. I tracked pines and cedars killed by salt, far up Shepherd Spring Creek and the Pinhook River, Money Bayou, and the backsides of the islands. I tabulated declines in the annual Christmas Bird Counts.

I am not native to the northern Gulf of Mexico. I was raised near the New Jersey shore. But each of us is fully indigenous to the Earth. No matter the bioregion of our origin, injuries our species has perpetrated against our planet's climate and biodiversity grieve us. We may not know with scientific precision the extent of the wounds that pierce and accumulate, but we live with the loss. We know our beaches and our oceans, our neighborhoods and our trees grow quiet. All living things have language. They demonstrate with their bodies and their voices what they have to say. What the wild animals and the wild islands are telling us is this: you leave us no place to live.

How can we change the trajectory of these losses? I have posed this question to scientists, to birdwatchers, to lovers of sea turtles, to activists, and to therapists. I listened for stories from the coast and its creatures. I have studied the cultural assumptions that allow this destruction to occur. I prayed for dreams to guide me.

NOT LONG AGO I dreamed about a woman wearing a ceremonial cape pieced together from the feathers, skins, and bones of wild animals. Her garment was a crazy quilt, fashioned of white beach mouse fur, the plumes of an oystercatcher, and the pelage of a fox squirrel, attached to a helmet constructed from the bony skull and long bill of a brown pelican. A buffalo skin formed the back of the cloak. Woven throughout were tiny flowers of an endangered plant called butterwort. Bits of ancient clay pottery served as fastening buttons.

At first I could find no comfort or direction from the dream. But as I thought about the long past of our coastline and its uncertain future, my night reverie became a helpful teaching and a guide for this book. It reminded me that in each fragment is the shape of the whole, and that my task was to unearth and stitch together what I could of the stories of the coast, and of the animals and people who have lived here.

My hope in bringing together the stories in this book is to reconstitute something like the cape in my dream, to warn us and guide us as we ride this coastline we love so dearly into an uncertain future. Some of the stories describe extinction of land, climate, and beings; others simply reflect the beauty and wonder I have seen. The stories may seem fragmented, not smooth and unbroken like the surface of the sea. But maybe this is a true thing, how we live in this time, trying to find our way back to wholeness.

ALL MY LIFE, I have been coming to the coast. As a child, I lived with my family among the foothills of the northern Appalachians, about fifty miles from the New Jersey shore. I loved our leafy green town, but my geographical orientation was fixed due east toward the saltwater edge of the continent. My mother taught me to want the sea. If love and longing were enough to save the wild seacoasts, they would have remained unscathed.

On our frequent trips to the shore, we never talked about the landscape we traversed—the coastal plain that stretched between home and the Atlantic Ocean. No natural landmarks or stories guided us. We had only the hanging green directional signs along the Garden State Parkway to show us the way. No one ever mentioned how the land and the sea roll on deep waves of time, or anything about the ten thousand years humans had lived in relationship to this coast before us. My family wasn't alone in our ignorance about this place we nevertheless loved so dearly.

The towns of Seaside Park and Seaside Heights had been built on a slim and delicate twenty-mile long peninsula, very like the islands I love in North Florida today. It never registered in my mind when we traveled there that we approached an island and crossed over a tidal lagoon in order to reach our destination. I barely noticed the ribbon of Barnegat Sound underneath our car as we rumbled over the drawbridge. All of our attention was focused forward. We competed to catch the first sight of the sea. This could have been a moment to notice that the beaches belonged to the continent's barrier island system. What I learned instead was to follow my longing to be at the edge of the sea.

Although I was not taught the anatomy of the coast, my sister Bobbie and I had full-body experiences with Barnegat Bay, the lagoon that divided the island peninsula from the mainland. My sister and I were small and skinny. The water was black and bitterly cold. Blue crabs sidled between clumps of sea grass on the bottom. If you stood long in one place, your toes would work their way down through the seaweed, and you might get pinched.

The part of Long Beach Island that once had been natural dune and swale had been flattened, plotted into grids, and then covered over with beach-house communities. Every family we knew had their preferred place to visit at the shore. Our next-door neighbors, the Grambors, always drove to Mantoloking. The Ciandellas liked Sea Bright, and it was understood that the Guldens would summer at Lavallette. Middle-class shore towns—their streets and houses and stoplights—were undifferentiated and continuous. Only highway signs let you know when you had crossed from one community into the next. We never visited a salt creek, a shorebird rookery, an Indian midden, or an offshore bar.

Once we arrived at the public beach of Seaside Heights, we trudged between the rental cottages, hobbled by towels, lemonade, a paper sack of peanut butter sandwiches, and one aluminum beach chair for my mother. From her seat on the sand, she watched so that we did not venture too far into the cold, indigo Atlantic. You could not see her eyes nor read her mood behind her mask of sunglasses and Kent cigarettes, but I knew my mother would be staring beyond our play, in the direction of her own private longings. Time at the beach helped my mother contain the extremes of her life. She oversaw the happiness and safety of her children and, at the same time, looked to the impossible horizon of her unarticulated dreams.

It was the 1950s, and then the 1960s, and our family was part of the middle-class metropolitan population with enough leisure time to go to the beach for fun. Gas was plentiful and cheap; boxy station wagons that could accommodate big families were affordable; rail lines allowed my father to commute back and forth to Manhattan on the rare occasions we rented a cottage for a week. Proximity to New York and Philadelphia had led to the establishment of resort communities such as Atlantic City, Asbury Park, and Wildwood, during the first two decades of the twentieth century.

The level of greenhouse gases in the atmosphere was three hundred parts per million and rising, but we knew nothing at all about that. Instead, corporate marketing taught us what we wanted, and television convinced us what we needed to buy.

What I am saying is that we—an entire population—had no concept of the beach as part of a natural system, or the atmosphere of the Earth as a whole. We simply drove to the edge and got out of the car. That was what we knew, the front beach—and the bright lights of the boardwalk, of course.

We did learn something of the habits of the coquina and the sand flea. As children we occupied the same shifting place on the sand. I knew that small fish and crabs lived in the trough behind the breakers, because we sometimes found them with our feet. We were familiar with laughing gulls and sandpipers (our catch-all name for all of the other shorebirds), and we knew the ghost crabs that dodged our dogs. But for the most part, we were preverbal and primitive in our understanding of our relationship to the landscape that we traversed and the coastal beings with which we shared it.

Still, my parents gave me a great gift: abundant time to play and swim by the ocean. The shore is a regenerative and healing place for the human spirit, and children are resilient. We rolled in the hot sand and buried each other. We dripped liquid sand through our fingers to make castles, floated in black inner tubes we had picked up at a gas station until we were sleepy or seasick, and jumped the waves until our mother said our skin had turned blue. In these ways, I learned the fundamental rhythms of the coast through my body. And I came to believe that my personal territory, no matter how far inland I lived, included the closest, wildest coastline.

Take away intention. I had none. Dismiss any thought of a plan. I drifted south after high school, drawn to the Gulf of Mexico. I didn't know enough to believe in my destiny, so the northern mountains had to shake me loose, down the eastern seaboard. Not yet knowing my place on the planet, I waited tables on the Outer Banks of North Carolina, worked for a time as a field technician on South Carolina's coastal plain, went to college in St. Petersburg and Gainesville, and finally found my way home to my life and my work in North Florida. Just as the Appalachian Mountains shed their rock to create the sandy coast I love, I believe they tumbled me down their long spine to the south.

THE FIRST TIME my husband, Jeff, and I visited Cabbage Top, that moment when I saw with my own eyes how the islands are slipping into the sea, I could have been lost in despair. No one could blame me if I had said to Jeff, "Let's not come back here anymore. I can't watch another place or species go down. It's just too sad."

How could we ask for respite from a place that was itself washing away?

But the island offered another point of view. A red cedar tree grew in the shade of the pines. It had pushed out creamy, mustard-yellow cones from the tips of its branchlets, bent on reproduction, no matter that the sand dissolved under its roots. Following the tree's crazy hope, rooted into impermanence, I knew we must likewise be steadfast in our love for these islands. Even though I wanted only to deeply experience the wild edge of this coast as it is and had been, I knew I had agreed to witness whatever comes to pass.

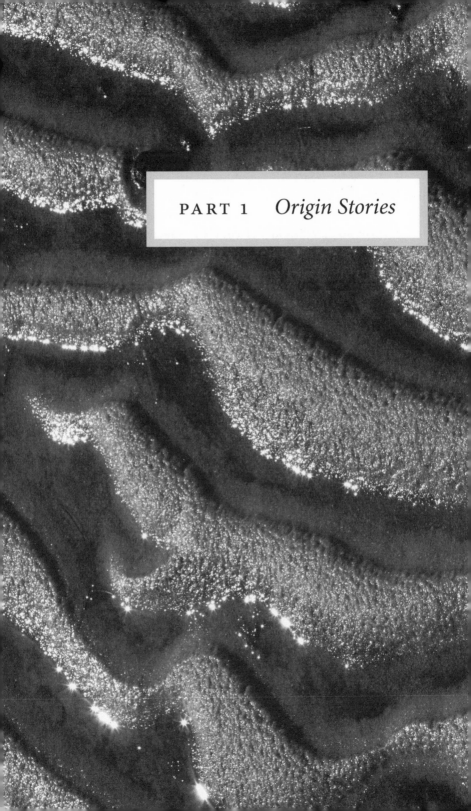

PART 1　*Origin Stories*

The body of the coast, from the youngest sand bar
to the oldest dune, records its evolution. I made
a practice of learning about our barrier islands'
geological rhythms, the cycles and processes
that sculpted them. At first, I studied the parts
of the coast as if they were distinct entities. But
the beaches and bars, the passes and the sand
ridges, do not, cannot, exist independently of
one another. And each habitat shelters a unique
and particular set of wild creatures and botanical
communities. As I tried to comprehend the nature
of the islands more deeply, the question in my
heart was this: how do we find the courage to
live on the edge of certain impermanence, and
yet never give up trying to fiercely protect these
beautiful inventions of the Earth?

CHAPTER 1

Sand Supply

"WHO MADE THE WORLD?" asks Mary Oliver in her poem "The Summer Day." "Who made the swan, and the black bear?"

Who made the coast? I have wondered. This particular coast, these saintly islands, these powerful passes, these bounteous life forms?

A mountain-born river is the answer.

If you look at a satellite photo of Florida's panhandle between Bald Point and Panama City, your eye cannot miss the channel that has delivered our shoreline's sediment. For 2 million years, quartz sand weathered from Appalachian rock washed down the Chattahoochee and the Flint rivers. At their confluence, the Apalachicola River carried the sand down to the Gulf of Mexico and opened like a fist, showering and shaping ground-up mountain into a broad, blunt-tipped arrowhead. Over many eons, the river punched through its own accumulations, growing out the land.

But the birth of the barrier islands required something even more than this enormous supply of sediment: a slowly rising sea to push back against. That time came about eighteen thousand years ago, at the end of the Pleistocene Ice Age. The planet's ice caps and glaciers were slowly melting as the Earth warmed. Sea level rose, and the Gulf Coast shoreline receded into its present position. By about four thousand years ago, the Apalachicola was delivering sediment faster than coastal wave energy could sweep it away. At the same time, the climate stabilized and the rate of sea-level rise accordingly slowed. Conditions were perfect for the deposition of sediment into a barrier rim.

As the sand accrued, it formed a circlet around what we now call Apalachicola Bay, the configuration of our present-day coast.

First St. Vincent, and then St. George and Dog Islands and the St. Joe spit began to build upward from the sand and clay cupping the river's mouth.

Two thousand years before the present, the islands had nearly approached their modern positions and were still growing in area and elevation. A larger sand supply led to higher, wider St. Vincent Island. Smaller depositions of sand fueled lower, narrower St. George and Dog, swimming like serpents in the sunset sea.

Tremendous sand banks still fringe our coastal islands, trapping and hoarding the sediment the land uses to remold itself. You can see the bars at low tide, especially during the winter months when new moon and north wind collaborate. Under these conditions I like to watch the astonishingly naked arm of sand that sprawls in five long banks from the western tip of St. Vincent Island, and points like an arthritic forefinger—each joint, each sandbank, slightly off kilter—toward Cape San Blas. A very good chance to commit its humps and narrow breaches to memory for future boating, I think to myself, when I see that rarely exposed sand.

In the fall nearly a thousand brown pelicans, intermixed with lesser quantities of cormorants, skimmers, and terns, rest and regroup on St. Vincent's breaching bars. But not a single one of those birds spends the night there. The pelicans organize into brief skeins of ten or fifteen at sunset and flap away to the east. Evenly spaced and entrained to one another, they lift and lower over gentle hills of warm air I cannot see. They do not fish or dive as they travel. I have heard that they retreat to an isolated sand bank off the far end of St. Vincent, where they will not be disturbed by raccoons, wild pigs, or people. I wanted to know that place.

One morning, Jeff and I nosed our motorboat through a break in the sandbar and cruised east along vast St. Vincent, following the path of the birds. The bright sun tensed my eyes in a squint.

"What's that on the horizon?" asked Jeff, pointing out a wavering, toothy profile emerging on the horizon. At first it was impossible to make sense of what broke the flat line between sky and sea.

We knew it wasn't Little St. George, the next island in the chain. Its tip stood firm to our left. I peered harder through my binoculars, and the mirage revealed itself.

"It's the pelicans! They are standing on a bar!"

Sure enough, as we neared West Pass, the silhouettes of birds sharpened. We approached the delta from the Gulf side, giving lots of berth to the semipalmated plovers, sanderlings, and black-bellied plovers loafing at either tip. In widely spaced groups, brown pelicans slept hard against the sand. A line of twenty bathed on an ankle-deep spit. We ran our boat along the considerable length of the bar—a mile maybe—with a bulge and a hook at each end. Near the skinnied-out center of the islet, taking care not to flush the birds into flight, Jeff steered ashore. I set the anchor on a short leash and dug its points into the sand. Then we stepped from the boat and walked.

At its greatest height, the island stood no more than a foot above the level of the sea. Small ghost crabs scuttled about the sloughs. Where the sand swelled highest, a few clumps of shrubby beach elder hunkered about to our knees. Wind-blown sand had filled in around their roots, using the plants as sand fences to build tiny new dunelets.

"This looks like a barrier island in the making," said Jeff. "See how its profile undulates? It's almost a mimic of St. Vincent's' dunes and swales. But this one isn't a newly forming island. This sandbar is actually what is called an ebb tidal delta, a great big one."

The pelicans had led us to the easternmost of the island's companioning deltas. Jeff pointed toward West Pass, the major outlet between Little St. George and St. Vincent. When tidal currents rush in and out of the mouths of passes, they relax their hold on some of the sediment they carry. The sand volume stockpiled in bars outside West Pass was phenomenal.

"In fact," mused Jeff, "There may be more sand in this delta than in one of the nearby islands. And since the Apalachicola River has been dammed upstream, 'new' sand is no longer delivered from the mountains." Deposits like these are all that remain to furnish our islands with the raw material to rebuild and recover from erosion, and allow them to keep pace with sea-level rise.

THE SANDBAR was a place for storing precious sand, yes, but evidence of its night-roosting birds equally entranced me. Barefoot, we picked our way between splatters of quarter-sized guano. It looked as if the sky had hurled white sticky hail at the ground.

I could see how recently the sand had been pocked and probed, as if the island's temperature had been measured by hundreds and hundreds of beaks and bills. Where birds had strutted or stood still to preen, the ground was stamped in little patterns of chained footprints. And every bit of the damp sand clutched feathers: the swift flight feathers of terns, enormous quilled pelican plumes, and, everywhere, a sifting of fluffy down. Pinions for contour and color, feathers to bristle and signal, plumage for propping and warming and digesting. Even the beach elders were stuck all over with the tiniest flakes of feathers, like miniature Christmas trees ornamented with down. Was this island growing feathers or shedding them?

I sat on the damp bar and contemplated the enormous, plume-embellished delta. It reminded me of a fairytale my father had read to me when I was a girl, about an imprisoned princess set to impossible tasks by her evil stepmother. For one of the challenges, she was brought great baskets brimming with feathers plucked from every kind of bird—nightingales, canaries, larks, doves, thrushes, peacocks, magpies, parrots, owls, eagles, and many, many more. All of these were shuffled together in such confusion that even the birds themselves could not have selected out their own. The stepmother commanded her prisoner to sort the feathers and arrange them according to species by the set of the sun, fully certain she would fail. The princess began to work, but before she had taken up a dozen, she realized that it was perfectly impossible to know one from another.

I picked up a handful of feathers from the sand and arranged them in a circle around me. I felt so privileged to visit that night-time refuge of wild birds, that repository of mica-flecked, mountain-shed sediment. But as I stroked a single chocolate, angled plume, watching and feeling it vibrate in the wind, I realized it wasn't these feathers I wanted to sort and identify, but the barrier island coast and all its parts, and the human story in relationship to it.

After a time, we left the delta and returned in our boat to Indian Pass, where we would spend the night. A storm blew in from the Gulf. Rain came pecking and pummeling, and I pressed my face against the sliding glass door of our rental house to watch. Lightning daggered through the thunderheads, igniting campfires within the bodies of the clouds and illuminating the island across the pass. I imagined birds standing out on that bar—pelicans and terns, willets and whimbrels—squeezing shut their eyes to keep out the driving rain. Perhaps they shifted their small weights from foot to foot, pressing their tracks deeper into the sand. I thought for a long time about them and how, to be safe, shorebirds must choose the barest outposts of sand, remote discontinuous bars, so that predators cannot surprise them as they sleep.

In my childhood fairytale, a magical prince appeared to rescue the princess. With three taps of his wand, the millions of feathers arranged themselves in scant heaps, each belonging to a different bird. Nothing magical will protect the wild birds nor insure the existence of the coast we so love. That will come only with our own human effort and understanding.

CHAPTER 2

Front Beach

ON A BRISK February afternoon, I settled my spine against a sand dune and watched the Gulf throw bolt upon bolt of fine silk at the shore. River sediment tinged the waves latte. When that suspended clay and sand is deposited on this shore, new dunes can grow. I dug my hands into the gentle sand, freckled with black. It clung to my fingers, soft grained, finer than granulated sugar, but not as fine as confectioner's. I poured the cool granules from my left hand into my right. The Appalachian Mountains once stood as tall and rugged as the Rockies are today. Over millions of years, those granite peaks weathered into two main components—milky white quartz and dark feldspar—and sluiced down the river. I held the bodies of mountains in my hands.

St. Vincent Island's gulf beach is vast, much wider and more durable than the others in our barrier chain, at least a hundred paces from dune to saltwater edge. The shore appears as if it had been bulldozed, but it is the wind and tide that rasp and shovel the sand, devising exceedingly subtle variations on the concept of flat. Small, low-energy waves grumble against the shore, each bearing a load of river sediment to further build out the beach.

"The Gulf beach at Saint Vincent is very much to our mind," wrote zoologist William Hornaday in 1909. "For 10 miles or more you can swiftly drive upon it a la Ormonde, and the wheels of your beach-wagon will scarcely leave a mark upon the hard-packed sands. The long stretch of south shore is rapidly building seaward, and the process of beach-making, and forestation of it, first with beach grass, then with long-leafed pine and palmetto, is one of the most interesting sights of the island."

Hornaday also reported that "the beaches are well stocked with gulls and shorebirds, of many species, some of which I could not positively identify without committing murder." But I rarely see shorebirds along this beach in quantities I would call "well stocked." On a long walk during the colder months, I might encounter three or four small fleets working the water's edge, each typically including a dozen or so red knots, a few willets, a half-dozen ruddy turnstones, a contingent of sanderlings, a black-bellied plover.

In proper season, you can also find some of the rarest of our rarest shorebirds—Wilson's, piping, and snowy plovers—along this front beach. You have to look carefully, but all three species (plus a more common relative, the semipalmated plover), make themselves known by peeling away from the water and racing inland when they are disturbed. In the warm months, snowy and Wilson's plovers nest on the mid- to upper beach, well beyond the zone that the high tide visits each day. Along narrow stretches of Dog and St. George Island, the birds must nest behind the first line of dunes.

Through my binoculars I watched a tiny muffin of a bird—some variety of plover—scurry up the rising ground, toward the dunes. The breeze carried it over the sand, weightless as a dried strand of seaweed. The fast scramble of its legs seemed irrelevant to its forward motion, so lightly was the bird strung on its bones. Tiny puffs of sand exploded from under its feet as it ran against the wind. The wind blew so hard that the plover paused to hunker in the wake of anything that might break the gust. I spotted a second plover taking dubious shelter behind a chunk of clay. Plovers' backs are the same soft brown as river mud, and their faces are as pearly as the planet Venus set in a black velvet sky. In breeding plumage, both snowy and piping plovers are marked with black brow lines, as if anointed by the quick stroke of a brush. A dark band encircles the necks and upper chests of the Wilson's and the semipalmated. The sun focused enough light for me to note a thin black bill (eliminating the Wilson's, with its large, stout bill) and a pale, incomplete collar. A snowy plover.

The movements of the plovers led my eye to the very edge of the beach, where birds dodged the incoming waves and dipped their bills into the backwash. I watched a larger shorebird, a willet, pluck a coquina clam from the wet sand. The coquina has mastered life on the edge, just as the shorebirds have. With a single muscled foot, the clam digs down quickly between waves to maintain a position just above the tide.

I thought about a time the previous summer when I lay in the surf among a host of those colorful coquinas, trying to sense myself into their experience. The waves sifted salt water and sand between my toes and the strands of my hair. I had to pay close attention to each incoming breaker, or it would fill my mouth, as well as my eyes and ears. The water scoured the sand from beneath my body, undermining my limbs as the substrate turned momentarily liquid. When the frothy bubbles subsided, I had just a moment to watch the small clams all around me stand on one end and bury themselves. Where there had been hundreds of pastel coquinas, I could see only small dimples in the sand.

No eyes or ears inform the coquina as it surfs the edge of the sea. It responds to the constantly changing environment with its entire sensate body, especially its muscled foot and two siphons. Side by side at the edge of the sea, our experience of life is so different, me and the coquina clam. Both of us are in constant dialogue, but unlike me the coquina attends and responds only to its surroundings—the consistency of the sand and the drag of the water. My active mind, with all its desires and fears, sometimes marginalizes the sensory input from my body. Too often I unconsciously retreat from directly experienced reality; my mind chatters endlessly with itself. But when I sit in the surf zone, I can feel how wet salt droplets fill the air and blow onto my skin, so that no matter how much water actually covers my body I am utterly submerged in this place. This is how it feels, living on the edge.

THE EPHEMERAL SAND of the front beach is not only nursery ground, essential nursery ground for coquinas and a dozen species of shorebirds and seabirds, but also for sea turtles—four kinds. One hot August day, the nest of a threatened species—the loggerhead sea turtle—rested at the bottom of the hole I excavated with rubber-gloved hands.

The ground was densely packed. I hauled out handfuls of the coarse-grained beach until I had created a vertical posthole so deep that I had to lie flat, cheek to grit, up to my shoulder in the sand.

"You are about to run out of arm," quipped one of my guides, a tall, genial firefighter named Mike. His wife, Robin, one of St. Vincent Island's most devoted volunteers, was in charge of the nest-check expedition. Mike and I had already watched Robin carefully excavate the morning's first two nests. She had taught us in the way of all good instructors: demonstrate, then let the student learn by doing.

A foot and a half down, the hole began to fill with cool water. The texture of the sand became looser, almost fluffy. This signaled that I'd reached the egg chamber, Robin told me. My fingers encountered something saggy and sloppy, like a piece of old skin. I pinched it between my thumb and forefinger and dragged it to the surface. It was a castoff eggshell, tough like soft leather yet pliable. A perfect temporary container.

I hauled the nest contents up onto the beach, sorting spent shells in groups of ten and by category. A ripped empty skin indicated the successful hatch of a baby sea turtle. Of those, I had seven rows of ten, plus one: seventy-one baby turtles emerged from this hole. Next, I counted thirty eggs that had failed to hatch ("Which is not so bad," assured Robin, sensing my disappointment at so many unfulfilled lives). There were no live or dead hatchlings to tally, nor any sign of eggs ravaged by predator.

Robin pierced one of the unhatched golf ball-sized eggs with a pocketknife. Pop. Stink. A liquid aerosol of rot emerged from the shell, followed by an ooze of lemon-yellow curd.

"But look here," said Robin, extracting something solid from the mess. Mike and I held our noses, but gathered close to examine a very small turtle embryo, tiny enough to nestle in a teaspoon.

"This one died early in its gestation," Robin told us.

The miniature animal had all the parts of a turtle, including a pink and black shell curved to fit the arc of its egg, just so. Tiny ebony flippers wrapped around a beach ball of yoke, as if the animal hugged its own private Earth. At the time it died this was true; yolk and the enforced crescent of its shell were everything the turtle-that-wasn't-to-be would ever experience of the living world.

EARLIER THAT MORNING, Robin and Mike had met me at the refuge's rubber jet dock on the mainland and piloted across the pass in a government-owned Mako powerboat. Then we transferred our gear to a two-person "club" car. As the extra passenger, I sat in the middle, on the plenty warm cover of the cart's battery. We rattled nine miles down the shady spine of the island to its western tip. The sandy road had recently been surfaced with oyster shells, making for a bumpy ride, but we traveled faster than I'd ever be able to go on my bike. Best of all, we outran the notoriously dreadful yellow flies and mosquitoes that rule St. Vincent from April until first frost—usually sometime in December.

We broke out onto the beach at West Pass and worked east alongside the shimmering, khaki-brown Gulf. Our task was to dig up and inventory any nest overdue for hatching.

"Since we run daily volunteer patrols, we know exactly when each nest was laid," said Robin. "Sixty days is what you see in the literature for a loggerhead sea turtle nest. So we try to inventory each nest at about seventy days, no later than seventy-five days, if it hasn't already hatched."

The nests were marked by squat wire cages and yellow signs on stakes that read, "Do Not Disturb, Sea Turtle Nest." Mike began each dig by dislodging a thick layer of sand off the wire lips of a three-foot-square cage that had kept out hogs, raccoons, and coyotes.

"Those guys don't pay one bit of attention to our signs," he grinned, referring to those midsized predators. "So we designed the dimensions of the cage to be just larger than the reach of the average raccoon's forearm." Mike and his wife—blonde, supremely organized Robin—struck me as an inseparable team.

Near Rio Road, we came upon a grove of cabbage palms leaning low over the water, and found a turtle nest exposed to the surf, like the ancient shell middens that pock the back side of the islands. Three eggs actually rested on the surface of the sand—no turtles survived or hatched out there. The combination of an exceptionally high, full moon–induced tide and a big storm two days prior (so intense that a waterspout knocked out the power to nearby St. George Island for days) did this nest in, Robin and Mike surmised. They told me about the effects of Hurricane Dennis, a Category 3 storm that pushed up many meters of storm surge all along this coast in 2005. The day after Dennis, Robin was right back out checking nests. She found eleven false crawls—basically U-turns in the sand. So much sand had been washed away by the storm that mother turtles could not find safe places to nest. "Where did the dunes go? Where is our beach?" they must have wondered.

"Still, the island has recovered and rebuilt since Dennis, with amazing vigor," said Robin. She pointed to a line of waist-high dunes corseted with railroad vines and even some sea oat clumps.

"I never thought I'd see this again after that storm," she continued. "Many of our foredunes were flattened and washed out to sea, and in their places we had small mountains of plastic junk marooned by the storm."

Farther down the island, south of Rattlesnake Road, a nest laid on June 3 told a very different story. The nest was situated on a low dune far above the wash of the water, at the base of a saw palmetto. Tough fibers of roots threaded through it. How did the mother dig this hole?

"She worked hard," said Robin, imagining the mother turtle's labor as she plowed her hands into the hole and through the fluffy nest chamber. "This is one huge nest." One by one, Robin lined up the discarded shells of 126 hatchlings, the day's largest haul, by far. She found 14 unhatched eggs, but none had been depredated. The wire cages had done their job.

But then she hauled out seven tiny corpses with heart-shaped, shrunken skulls. "Nature . . ." she said, waving away her unexpected tears, and ever so quickly orienting back to the practical.

"We're just lucky it's not hot. The rotting flesh of these baby turtles could make you pretty nauseous and bring in the flies in droves."

Robin was passionate about St. Vincent Island, its endangered species in particular. Her path to advocacy lay in a fierce dedication to the protocol of collecting good data.

"This is what we are here for. This is the gold," she said, totaling the numbers from the nest in her head. I wondered if she believed she must hide her heart to be taken seriously by refuge managers and other scientists.

And then, a miracle: Robin disengaged a live hatchling from the nest hole. He was dehydrated and coated with sugar sand, but he squirmed in her fingers, fully alive. We were enchanted. It had been seventy days since this nest was laid. Ten days may have passed since this little one's living siblings dug themselves out and left him in the underground nest turned tomb. Marine biologist Dr. Anne Rudloe once described to me how at the end of the two months' incubation, sea turtle hatchlings churn to the surface en masse, the sand falling beneath their bodies, the nest essentially working its way to the surface. The turtle babies run a race against time from the moment of hatching, and this one almost lost.

Robin laid him gently on the beach and continued her work. I rushed to the Gulf and dipped up a cup of seawater to wash the sand from his eyes. A good third of that creature was head, which he began to buck, as if to toss sand from his upward path, a motion he must have employed to exhaustion before his unexpected release. He lifted his head, looked around, and his berry black eyes, sunk deep in protective sockets, locked onto the enormous stretch of water he would swim in the rest of his life.

Robin shook another hatchling free of the deep sand. Mike and I sat back on our heels and admired the two babies as they stretched their tiny necks from reticulated cowls of skin, sensing their path to the sea. It was important to allow them to complete the journey to the water by themselves. Scientists have learned that when baby sea turtles leave their nest beach, they absorb and imprint on essential chemical cues from the sand. If one of these was a female and managed to survive two or three decades in the open sea until she was sexually mature, with strength and luck she will return to dig her own nest right here, within a few feet of where she was hatched. I watched the small turtles toboggan downslope and push with curved front flippers, thin, like wings, against the inches-high uphill terrain. They seemed so frail, but filled with a will to complete their encoded journey to the Gulf.

I hummed a prayer to the turtles as I watched two tiny tail nubs and two sets of filigreed back flippers disappear into a mild foamy wave. I longed for one last look. There it was: A baby turtle broke the surface with its little head once, twice, and again, as it swam through the surf zone, then breaststroked away into the broad Gulf.

Thrive and return, I thought. May you thrive and return to our sand.

CHAPTER 3

Relict Ridges

FOUR OR FIVE thousand years ago, St. Vincent—the oldest island in our barrier chain—was just a crescent of sand, much like the sandbars that guard the inlets. How many countless times the island-to-be must have disappeared under high and moon-enhanced tides, and reemerged at low tide, before it could finally believe in its own existence. Everything that would ever live here had to wait for that first beach ridge to emerge. But as soon as the sand did drain and dry and pile above high tide, plants did their part. Large grains of sea oats and sandspur—whole seed banks of colonizers—blew in on currents of air or were floated from other beaches and began to dress the dunes. The river supplied sediment, feeding and fattening the island, and then coquinas and ghost crabs, snowy plovers and sea turtles laid their eggs and extended the range of their kind. After a ridge was well established above the level of the Gulf, wind built it even taller. Quantities of sand were dropped and sculpted atop each ridge in a process beautifully named aeolian decoration. All of this came to pass in super slow motion relative to our limited human perspective.

From a satellite photo, you can see that St. Vincent is curiously combed with fine white lines. Like rings that build outward on a tree, these parallel streaks—called beach ridges—are the remnants of miles-long lines of dunes stranded inland as the island built out into the Gulf of Mexico.

When I imagined St. Vincent's origins, I assumed it had been carved from the mainland and then cut off and stranded in the Gulf by the river-fed lagoon and the passes. I thought this would account for the island's apparently perfect replication of mainland plant communities: pine forests, scrubby sand ridges, jungly live-oak hammocks, and freshwater ponds, marshes and sloughs.

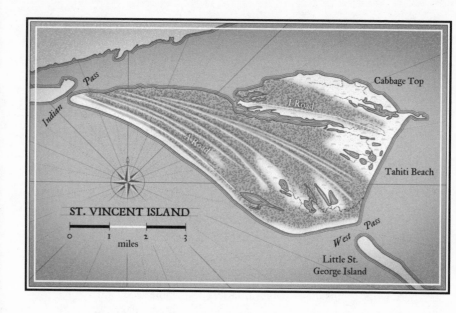

But water and wind and plants constructed this island, one ridge at a time. Each is an echo of its neighbor, and each is an ancient shoreline, the remains of a very old beach. The northernmost hummock (closest to the mainland) is the oldest and the lowest, less than three feet above sea level. The knolls immediately adjacent to the Gulf are the youngest (some as tall as twenty feet). The others fit in order of age and height between the two. Dog Island, the two St. Georges, and St. Joseph Peninsula also have developed at least a few beach ridges. But on St. Vincent, the downstream recipient of the Apalachicola River's sediment load, scientists have tallied more than a hundred ridges that have advanced the size of the island over the last four thousand years, pleating its surface like a cockleshell. The mounds piled up in hills of sand shaped like the mild combers or waves that bring the sediment ashore, one about every eighty or ninety years, about the span of a long human life. At times when the sea level was either

falling or stable, sand accumulated (which scientists call prograd-
ing), and the island grew more quickly. When sea level was rising,
progradation rates were lower. The dozen sets of beach ridges pre-
served on St. Vincent Island offer a physical chronology, an unusually complete and well-preserved record of the island's response
to the beat of the surf, the rise and fall of the tide, and the flow of
sand, through time.

CHOOSE A WINTER'S DAY to walk backward through time
across St. Vincent, because in summer, biting insects will not
respect your desire to linger. Their lives require warm and cours-
ing mammalian blood. Walk down the shore to Road 2, and turn
inland, up the beach. The bare sand is textured and pocked by
wind and rain. Storm waves or exceptionally high tides sweep
the landscape flat every year or two. As you cross the wide upper
beach and the newly forming dune line, you will notice that it
has been colonized by salt-tolerant plants. Two morning glory
sisters—railroad vine and beach morning glory—lay down tracks
over the sand, unreeling thirty feet or more across the beach
like lengths of brown twine, but pink and living at their growing
tips. The flowers of railroad vine come purplish pink in the fall.
Blowing sand quickly fills in around the sparse and shy stems
of the white morning glory. Their flowers—small crenellated
moons, improbably thin and fragile—seem to spring directly
from the hot sand, each paired with a single thickened leaf.
Wasps and flies, big and small, striped and plain, back in and out
of their lemon-yellow centers.

 Plants that succeed a bit farther up the beach are mostly grasses
like sea oats, whose upward growth can keep pace with sand
burial. Their stems sift the wind, slowing its momentum and forcing it to drop the sand grains carried across the beach. In this way,
the grasses promote the habitat they like to live on. Windblown
grit accumulates around their roots. Together the plants and sand
grow upward to form a new dune.

As you mount the low, steep dunes, you will want to pause and absorb the soundscape. Behind you, waves murmur as they crease against the sand, and shorebirds and seabirds call. You might see a brown pelican or a Forster's tern glide over the pine forest, but it will fly silent over the trees. In the pine canopy you can hear the complex burble of bluebirds, the zing of blue-gray gnatcatchers, and the fussing of nuthatches. These are terrestrial birds; you don't expect to see or hear them at the beach.

As you skate down the dune's backside, widely spaced slash pines and cabbage palms shade your path. Instantly, the sea wind will break. A great ocean of yucca, sea oats, lupine, and seeding grasses blanket this swale. In late spring, the lupines will fill the interdunal space with spiring purple magnificence. If you watch for a while, you can almost see them straighten their heavy flower stalks, offering themselves to their pollinators. In November, brilliant senecio asters will take the place of the lupines, serving the nectaring needs of monarch and Gulf fritillary butterflies.

Continue along the path and you will climb a meter in altitude up a second beach ridge into a fairyland of drought-adept plants. A desert mosaic of dwarf oak, cactus, rosemary, a carpet of lichen, and bare glittering sand crown this ridge. Fragrant, evergreen-needled rosemary resembles the herb cultivated for flavoring, but it is an entirely unrelated species. In October, lavender lanterns of scrub mint attended by clouds of monarch butterflies will light the path.

Walk farther. At the hem of the second old dune, slash pine flatwoods come edging. Beneath the pines, bouquets of big-finned saw palmetto crane to catch the light. At the lowest elevations, cradling the sky's fresh rainfall, narrow saw-grass sloughs bounded by button bush, red bay, and willow, snake the length of the island. Stringers of single-file cabbage palm mark these waterways, offering vertical perspective to your eye. At the eastern end of the island, the sloughs spread into lakes, which are favored resorts of wintering waterfowl and colony-nesting egrets and herons.

If you continue walking, you will catch on to the geological rhythm of the island, how each relict beach ridge, spaced thirty to three hundred feet from the next, is clothed in a plant community differently from the alternating wetland swales. You will notice how plants grow in obedience to the shape of the land according to its height above the water, the amount of salt spray it receives, and the sufficiency of organic matter accumulated in the soil.

St. Vincent Island is crosshatched with many miles of roads. If you tire of walking north, you can change direction and amble toward one end of the island or the other. These east–west roads, trapped between beach ridges, are gorgeous and monotonous artifacts of a hundred years of human activity, plowed and tamped with oyster shell, so the island's owners might hunt, clear-cut timber, and patrol for poachers.

Because the island is fretted like the neck of the guitar with roads, our own explorations of its interior tend to be linear. When I ride my bike, I feel as if my soft tires massage the bony vertebrae of the island's spine. On either side of me stretch long revetments of sand, ancient linear dunes. They look as if a child's hands had mounded and patted them into place. So fine and inviting are those long low dunes, ornamented with aromatic rosemary and white gleaming sand.

Only after a solid frost beats back the flies and mosquitoes do we venture off the island's beach. But on chilly days, we bike miles of island road, and then sprawl on some old dune deep in the heart of St. Vincent, listening and watching for the endangered red wolves that are bred here. Above our heads, we look into layers and layers of space. Stiff handspreads of palmettos shudder in the winter breeze. Even higher, collars of grape and poison ivy muffle the necks of the pines. "Nee-ee-e-ah," whinnies a yellow-bellied sapsucker. I find it with my binoculars, clinging upside down to a clutch of poison ivy berries. The sun lights the ivy and grape leaves into stained glass—ruby and gold. I watch the bird gobble the white waxen fruit. Higher above the canopy, a sulfur butterfly, three adult eagles, and a Forster's tern sweep across my field of view. Each creature moves within a range of home and purpose I can only guess at, and yet I am joyful just to see them pass, in cameo. And I can feel how the island's rich life holds me, with all the others.

ROAD A runs the length of the island just behind the first beach ridge. Many creatures must be aware of my passage when I walk there, even though I see very few. I hear armadillos hop-plow through the saw palmetto, and I often spook a white-tailed deer or a sambar, a large exotic deer introduced to the island in 1908. I key into their tracks on trails and along the edge of marshes, and sometimes spot the broad browns of their flanks in the dappling woods. A rufous-sided towhee working through the palmetto is noisy enough to be mistaken for a foraging wild hog—until I hear its whistle.

The first time I reached the junction of Roads A and 4, what appeared as a simple triangle on the refuge map opened out into a long pond, one of five on the island. Coots, a tricolored heron, a great egret and an alligator swam or stalked away, shaken from their private lives by the squeal of my brakes. Beyond the pond rose small, exquisitely oaked dunes, and to the east there was a fine stand of pines and palms backlit by the azure sea and sky. I stopped, straddling my bike. It was like drinking clear water to stand and stare at all that beauty. I realized that the pond drains into what we call the boneyard creek, a freshwater outfall that flows right across the beach. Yet another piece of the island's geography fell into place in my mind.

Boneyards are common features on southern coastal islands like St. Vincent. You find them along stretches of beachfront where the sea is chewing back the forested land. In these places, it appears as if a crowd of palms and pines has crept close to the edge of the Gulf, and then been drowned or killed by salt. As powerfully as these slash pines grounded themselves so many years ago, they could not move with the shift of the sand. They have shed their bark. They have silvered into skeletons. Their crowns and their branches have tumbled free and stabbed into the sand. I run my hands over the exposed tripod-like architecture of one of the pine tree's roots. It resembles a stiffly radiating star. You could not guess at this belowground structure if the forest were still intact. Some of the cabbage palm understory of the boneyard forest still thrives greenly, but the death of the pines foretells its fate.

The boneyard we visit most often is carved through by a blackwater creek. I always wade upstream between four-foot sand cliffs threaded with palm roots like the bodies of earthworms. Overland flow combs them creamy and straight. Often I startle an enormous barnacle-backed blue crab or a school of small fish.

Alligators know this place, too. Sometimes I see their tail drags and the tracks left by their clawed feet, and I know they have traveled here, if not why. I imagine their scaled abdomens tractoring over the hot sand, and how they must hitch up their bellies to avoid a burn. The alligators must sense the settling trough of the creek somehow, the only place along the whole nine-mile Gulf front of St. Vincent where access to the freshwater wetlands is easy.

The creek is a place of balance, for the island retains no more water than her wetlands can absorb. When it rains hard, fresh water gathers in the long saw-grass sloughs and interior ponds and overflows into the Gulf through this sea-facing outlet. When drought comes, the boneyard creek shrinks to nothing at all. At the creek, I can almost feel the island's wetlands breathing in or letting go, depending on the rains.

If the day is warm, Jeff and I like to float at the interface of clear sweet water and milk chocolate Gulf before we leave the boneyard. Mullet leap and splash only feet from where we swim. Small sharks noodle in the surf. The creek is a way in, a promise of shade, a place where people may have once set up temporary camp. It has the aspect of a sea horizon with tall pines and fresh water, too. A place of anomaly and surprise. Perhaps it didn't exist when the original people came here, but there is someone who worships it now, and keeps it in her mind's eye, and that person is me.

Once I dreamed that I had come to the coast to meet with a group of biologists and administrators. In the dream, there were birds everywhere, including pairs of white pelicans swimming with featherless, nearly embryonic young. It was almost dusk. There wasn't time for me to go to the meeting and also investigate the birds. I made my choice, saying to my friends, "Let's go see where the pelicans are laying eggs and raising their chicks." The baby pelicans seemed to be emerging from a place where a little freshwater stream met the Gulf—my boneyard creek. In the dream, I carried a guidebook that explained, "The intersection of fresh creek and salt Gulf is where you go to look for the source, the laying, the creation."

I ROAD is an aged, still-standing rib of St. Vincent Island, nearly next in line to go back under the sea. One of the island's oldest beach ridges (after Cabbage Top and inaccessible H Road, to the north), I Road is flattening under three or four thousand years of its own mild weight.

Jeff and I made a plan to ride the I Road's four-mile spine from beginning to end. We transported our bicycles by boat to Big Bayou, where we offloaded them onto the island.

"This would be a glorious place to camp, wouldn't it?" I suggested, as we negotiated our bikes through a rough patch of yaupon holly toward the I Road. Enormous slash pines, lissome cabbage palms, and spreading live oaks stood shoulder to shoulder, on the western thumb of the road, creating a beautiful roof of shade. Troops of mosquitoes whined us an audible welcome.

"Not for very long!" Jeff replied.

We had in our minds the pleasant explorations of February, when insects still dreamed in their eggs and the sun wasn't yet pouring hot-sauce heat on our coast. But this was October, and so we dressed in layers to thwart the insects: long pants, T-shirts, and sleeved sun shirts, all tucked into socks and waistbands. Just as soon as I straddled my bike, clever flies snuggled in between my hat and my hair, humming a buzzy hunger. Through inborn instinct and long practice torturing the large mammals of the island, they aimed for the backsides of my ears and knees, and for the undersides of my wrists. I slapped them dead, rolling their fleshy bodies between my fingers, not so easy a task as I negotiated the rough, barely used road. One made the fatal mistake of flying into my mouth. I bit down and spat it back out.

What pulled us down the I Road, besides the always enticing Tahiti Beach at St. Vincent's east end? This: we traded the effort of our bodies for the thrill of knowing the island more deeply. For instance, the four pairs of great blue heron we had seen nesting in the last of the tall pines. Would those birds still be raising their young? And the tanagers, bluebirds, and nuthatches breeding in the pinewoods—already I could hear their songs and I was happy to know we were among them.

As we rode east, the dry land varied from only a few feet to several hundred feet wide, a bony, disintegrating finger of upland. When I stopped to drink water, my sneakers crunched down on the oyster shells dumped and spread to raise the level of the path. Even so, moisture crept between the seams of my shoes. The elevation of this beach ridge would need to be measured in inches, not feet, above sea level. One day, only the tamped shell tread of the road will remain, like a prop scar in sea grass, as the sand ridge sifts off into the rising tides.

There is no shade on the I Road, and the clouds of flies escorting us seemed to like it that way. In places, the path unrolled like an emerald meadow, but this wasn't a wide swath of woodland cloth—just two remnant ribbons with a road down the middle. The understory featured wiregrass clumps; saw palmettos, throwing out fleshy combs of celery-green flowering stalks; and a thickly blooming yellow aster. White-topped sedge, bog buttons, and yellow polygala told me that water often stood here. Brackish wetlands hemmed the road so closely that I startled a tiny rail swimming like a duck on open water. It fluttered into the marsh grass at my unexpected appearance.

Logging, rising sea level, and fire had pruned the ridge thoroughly. I rode under many fire-killed slash pines. For the most part, the oaks—such important habitat for migrating and breeding songbirds—had been burned back to the ground by prescribed fires allowed to burn too hot last season. Here and there remained a cluster of scrub live oak, and these were robustly accompanied by a palette of their dependent birds: pine, parula, and yellow-throated warblers; brown-headed nuthatches; and small woodpeckers. Those birds, I felt, would return to and ride the trees until they died from salt and silvered in the sun. And then, bald eagles and kingfishers would use the open frames of the dead pines to scan for prey.

The pines that flank I Road were no thicker than a spindly bottlebrush. Even the better ones could not compare to the awesome virgin stands described by William Hornaday, who visited the island in 1909 and left a vivid account of his impressions. "St. Vincent is covered with primeval forests of pines and palms, also some live oak, hickory and other trees," wrote the scientist, who was director of the Bronx Zoo. "The giant pines have never been cut or turpentined in the history of the island." But Hornaday knew that the timber industry was a mainstay of Florida's coastal economy, beginning as early as 1870. He wrote that "the mouths of the turpentiners and lumbermen actually water at the spectacle of all these millions of lovely pine trees, fairly bursting with No. 1 turpentine and yellow-pine lumber, all standing quite untouched."

St. Vincent's forests were spared for decades after the other islands and the massive coastal plain forests were timbered, due to the problem of transportation to the mainland and the desire of a string of uniquely conservation-minded owners to keep the island in its natural state. Today we look at a forest less than half regrown, a forest that was cut once in the 1940s, and then again in the early 1960s. In 1943 Malcolm Johnson wrote of the demise of the island forests in an article headlined "Loggers Invade Game Paradise to Fell War Timber." There is a photograph of the island taken after the second stripping of trees in the files of the refuge headquarters. You would not recognize the place. No shade is to be had. Cattle graze among saw palmetto beneath an unrelenting sun.

The I Road was mostly passable; we were only forced to dismount and lift our bikes over a couple of fallen pines. But I hated the way the trees sifted down just enough brown needles to disguise the road's sand traps, where the old dunes had dried out. My front wheel twisted and wobbled as it hit that sand, and I burned out my thighs and knees trying to power through to firmer ground. Then there were the places where wild pigs had torn up the surface and troweled the sand—same maddening story.

"Frack!" I yelled to Jeff's back disappearing down the road ahead as I ground to yet another halt. When my front tire bogged in the fine, deep sand, I got off the bike and waited until sweat and my racing heartbeat caught up with me. The four-mile ride was so grueling, I thought, maybe it was time for I Road to go ahead and dissolve into the sea, taking its load of biting insects with it.

When I caught up to Jeff, I said, "I'm feeling edgy about the possibility of running over a snake. They have nowhere else to go except this same narrow trail." We had already startled two black racers from the path, nothing venomous.

"I have been thinking about that, too," said Jeff, shaking off the circlets of insects making a go at his wrists. "And if anyone wondered why prehistoric people got off this coast and moved north between May and October, they should've been here today."

One of the ways my husband and I entertain each other when an expedition turns unreasonably grueling is to make a game of guessing who among our acquaintances could keep up with us. "We are tough!" Jeff likes to say. Often, we realize, it's not so much whether our friends could get through the trip we've designed, but why would they want to?

After dinner that night, my sister called to check in. "Where have you been all day?" she asked. "You didn't answer my calls." I described our I Road adventure. "It wasn't any pedal in the park," I admitted, naming the highlights of our itchy, sweaty, snake-wary trip.

"I figured you'd be doing something like that," she replied.

It was like childbirth, that steamy ride down the I Road escorted by biting flies. But once I reached Tahiti Beach, my struggle was forgotten. The island was again my friend, it was paradise, and I never wanted to leave. Small amethyst wavelets nudged a wide bed of shells against the beach, an overwashed lip of sand almost two miles long that seals the marsh behind it from the Gulf. Wind and salt had sanded the life from the front line of palms and oaks, but the beach was generously enticing. A southeast breeze beat the flies back inland. I sank against the sand under the shade of the palms, whose leaves glimmered, sifting the air as if it were fine flour. I gulped water, ate apples and almonds. Then I dissolved into pure stillness, synchronizing my pulse with that of the island, settling down from the hard push over the length of the land's old bone.

CHAPTER 4

Middens and Lagoons

THE BEST PLACE for oysters is where a river meets the sea, at the margin of salt water and fresh, and for this reason, Apalachicola Bay is acclaimed. But until the archipelago of islands became substantial enough to partially dam the bay, few or no shellfish were present. As the barrier rim amassed, circulation decreased in the estuary, and a perfect salinity came to be. Nutrient-rich sediments from deep in Georgia and Alabama fertilized not just islands, but a plentiful seafood nursery.

This abundance of protein attracted the Indians of the late Archaic Period about three thousand years ago and allowed them to establish themselves in the area. The early peoples adapted to the warmer climate, evolved a sophisticated use of coastal resources, and left behind a record of fired-clay pottery and stone tools. Their shell middens provide some of the oldest evidence of human presence in Florida's coastal zone. Along the northern shores of our chain of islands, several dozen mounds of shell erode into the lagoon, ranging in age from fifteen hundred to four thousand years old. The oldest of the known cultural sites are found on the northernmost beach ridges of St. Vincent Island. Others on St. George and Little St. George are younger, somewhere in the range of three hundred to a thousand years old.

One October afternoon, I joined Dr. Nancy White, an archaeologist from the University of South Florida, for a tour of Richardson Hammock on St. Joseph Peninsula. When you walk the short path from Stump Hole to the hammock, bright sand scalds your eyes and burns through the bottom of your shoes. No shade is offered by the saw palmettos, rosemary, scrub mint, or young pines that flank the path. Dry lichens form a bubbling

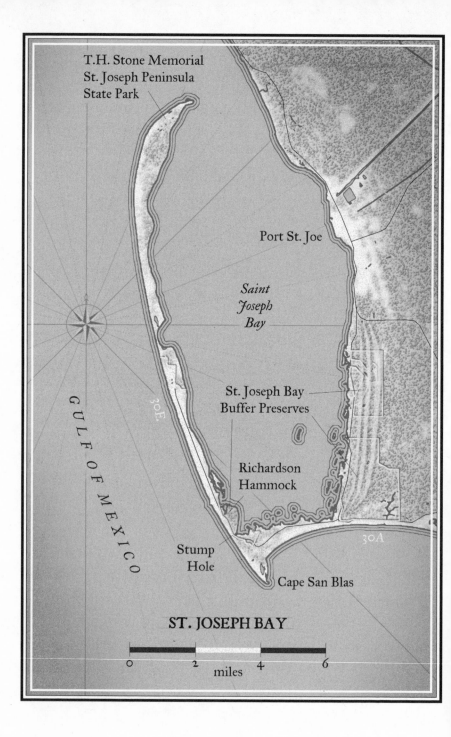

T.H. Stone Memorial
St. Joseph Peninsula
State Park

Port St. Joe

*Saint
Joseph
Bay*

St. Joseph Bay
Buffer Preserves

Richardson
Hammock

Stump
Hole

Cape San Blas

GULF OF MEXICO

30E

30A

ST. JOSEPH BAY

0   2   4   6
miles

fabric over the forest floor. Hidden away in the brush, rufous-sided towhees and catbirds whistle and scratch. Sweat trickles down your neck and pools in the small of your back. Breathing in, the resins of the plants are fragrant and bracing, but you cannot imagine living here.

As you round the trail, a thick green hillock blocks your view of St. Joe Bay. You are happy to move from the sun furnace of the thin pinewoods into this true Florida hammock, a hill raised high and tempered alkaline by two thousand years of shell refuse. But without a guide, you cannot imagine what lies under your feet.

The professor led us at a brisk clip, in full field garb: jeans, worn boots, a blue work shirt, and faded leather gloves. A green bandanna held long black hair and golden hoop earrings off her face. She carried a silver thermos on a sling over one shoulder and a red gear bag over the other. I liked her no-nonsense tone.

At the entrance of the hammock, Nancy gathered the group in close.

"Archaeology is the only social science where you don't need actual people to study, just their material evidence," she began.

"The questions we ask may seem simple, like when and why did people come here? How did they survive? Where did they find fresh water? What did they believe?" Nancy paused to let us contemplate. "The problem is that everything organic eventually rots. We have to piece together what happened thousands of years ago with so few clues. So our conclusions about how people lived can be quite biased.

"Still, we have found evidence of people from many time periods using this place," she continued. She didn't mean a couple of generations, our normal frame of reference in Florida when we talk about someone living here "a good long while." She was talking about three or four centuries of prehistoric camps at the edge of St. Joe and Apalachicola Bays.

We stood back as Nancy hacked a path through a cluster of yaupon holly with a substantial machete. She wanted to show us a site her team had excavated ten years earlier. I saw only a scattering of shells on the dark soil surface of the old dig site, which she described as a 1.5-by-2-meter rectangular trench.

"We found the most amazing features here," Nancy said. "For example, a cluster of sunray venus clamshells arranged in a carefully nested circle. People often express their prayers materially. Perhaps the shells represented gratitude, or a fervent wish. Or maybe the shells were used as kitchen tools, something like a set of linked measuring spoons. Or maybe they were simply a child's playful design," she added over her shoulder, as she forged through the woods. Soft branchlets of southern red cedar brushed our faces as we followed our guide, scrambling down a three-foot drop to the edge of the bay. My eyes squinted, adjusting to the sudden bright sunlight and the blue-gem brilliance of the water.

"Why did people camp right here, do you think?" asked Nancy.

"Because this was the first high ground next to the water?" someone guessed.

"That's it," she said. "Nice high dune ridge, waterfront access."

"But what did people do about mosquitoes?" asked a white-haired woman in khakis, batting at the flying pests around her face and neck. Among our group, the odor of insect repellant was strong.

"Simple," said our guide. "They didn't live here then. Nobody stayed near the coast during hurricane season. They'd move back up the rivers and creeks in their long cypress canoes. They were smart, and they knew the land and the weather!" She turned again to the shell midden behind us, sheared open like a layer cake by storm tides.

"We are looking here at an active area of erosion," she explained. "Organic waste from the ancient peoples is this charcoal color." With the tip of her machete, she nudged a horizontal black seam of soil that ribboned through the profile of the midden. To my eye, this midden resembled the compressed remains of a giant clambake, or in our part of the world, the mountains of oyster shells outside the seafood processing houses in Eastpoint.

"Where you see white layers, that's just sand, it's what we call 'culturally sterile,' with no embedded artifacts," said Nancy. She picked up a couple of worn gray conch shells that had tumbled free. She hefted them high, and then passed them among the group.

"This midden is different from the others on our coast. You'll notice lots of these horse conches and also lightning whelk shells. Those species were common in this salty bay—you don't see them so much behind St. Vincent or the St. Georges, where fresh water from the Apalachicola dilutes the bays' salinities."

In my mind, I started to piece together how the subtle differences in the land and waters selected what could live where, and how the first people, who lived with this coast so much longer than we ever will, knew exactly where to go to get what they wanted to eat.

Nancy gestured out toward the bay, transparent and aglitter in the late morning sun.

"Can't you just picture people wading with their kids in this shallow water to collect their dinner? Wouldn't that have been fun? Back here on the beach, it would be a simple matter to bash open the shells, and pick out the meat.

"Contrary to popular opinion, the lives of these early peoples were not nasty and brutish," the archaeologist said. "Studies of the few hunter-gatherer-fishers still living on Earth show that foraging isn't difficult, especially in resource-rich environments like this bay. You would have worked only three or four days a week gathering wild foods. The rest of the time was your own."

DOZENS OF VARIETIES of mollusks have been found in the shell middens left by prehistoric residents throughout the Apalachicola basin. People harvested a wide variety of seafood, although oyster shells predominate in the middens. It may be because those were the toughest shells and took the longest to deteriorate. And among the oyster shells, archaeologists find bones of fish and other animals that would have actually produced more meat than shellfish.

One of the experiences that makes me feel connected to the long ago peoples who lived at this coast is collecting scallops. Some years scallops come in thickest at St. Joe Bay, other times at Steinhatchee or Keaton Beach, or off the St. Marks Refuge. On a weekend it's easy to find a sweet spot—all you have to do is orient toward the cluster of boats with red dive flags aloft.

My feelings about scalloping are complicated. I love the purposeful hunt for food, and the full-body experience of finning through the amniotic salt water meadows. I love that pursuing scallops takes me floating in this vast natural aquarium, and how the long, raspy grasses brush against my skin. I love that the search for scallops isn't random. The animals choose their locations. Most lie nested in tawny hammocks of brown algae pocketed among the crisscrossing lengths of sea grass. It's my job to find the pattern in their choice of microhabitat.

But I do feel that the advantage is all ours. Millions of scallops are plucked from Florida's Gulf shallows on opening day alone, and the season runs from early July through the beginning of September. When you harvest scallops, you must harden yourself to the smile formed by their parted shells and the turquoise glitter of their exquisite, motion-detecting eyes. You shouldn't fail to give thanks as you take their lives from the sunny Gulf meadows.

Jeff raised a fluorescent orange diver's flag, and I clipped our bimini shade into place over the boat. We knew we would want to get out of the day's bright oven at lunchtime. To ward off sunburn, I wore a long-sleeved shirt over my bathing suit even though I was sorry to lose skin connection with the salt water. We tied net bags around our waists, adjusted masks and snorkels, and slipped over the side of the boat.

The first scallop I found sent a jolt of hunter-gatherer adrenalin through my body. Since the animal had not sensed my predatory intent, its two shells gaped about half an inch wide, allowing it to filter small particles of algae and organic matter from the water. A single scallop can pump through more than fifteen quarts of water in an hour—astonishing for a creature that seldom grows more than two inches in diameter. I grabbed the animal quickly, knowing it would spurt away if I was not fast enough, and turned it over in my hands. The scallop's sun-facing side was mossy green, coated with algae and other periphyton. The paired undershell had rested—snow-white—on the grass.

I pawed open my net bag, slid the scallop inside, and resumed the hunt. All around me, bright flat fish striped neon blue and yellow, only the size of my palm, twinkled among the grasses. When they turned on their sides to graze, the fish mirrored back the light as if each were a small golden sun. In this world there are always those who clean and glean, and we cannot do without them, nor can the sea. I stroked over a dip in the terrain. Sea grasses gave way to brown branching alga surrounding a patch of round sandy bottom. Here I found an abundance of scallops, thickly clustered and fitted into the sand and the vegetation. I plucked as many as my hands could hold before sliding them into my bag: two, three, four or even five at a time.

I didn't collect every scallop I found. Every now and then I encountered a wily individual that challenged me with its efforts to escape. Those I folded back into the grasses, urging them to prosper. "Stay hidden," I whispered. "Don't let the others catch you."

Although there were dozens of boats within shouting distance, the world underwater was silent, intimate, and uncrowded. I could only see a few yards ahead. The big horizon of the sky at the surface was lost to me. I meandered about on my quest and lost track of the cardinal directions, raising my head occasionally to orient to our boat. I listened to the rhythmic exhale of my breath through the snorkel, and to the clicks of scallops slamming shut their shells as they dodged my approach. Scallops are active swimmers, and they can move surprisingly quickly by clapping their two valves together and expelling water.

A mullet grazed at the edge of the sandy bowl. It seemed to feel safe in my presence, almost tame. It knew it was not my quarry and allowed me to snorkel along behind as it fed. As we swam through the sea meadow, I spied what looked like a vertical length of leather among the grasses. Somebody's lost belt, I wondered? But no, it was the tail of an enormous spotted eagle ray. The ray flashed into motion, as startled by me as I was by it. It was as long as the roof of my little car, yet I wasn't scared. I'd already escaped the strike of its barbed tail, and besides, the animal had no desire to harm me. Later I encountered another ray stirring up the bottom as it plowed a clear sandy stretch for things to eat. Again, the animal fled at the sight of me. I felt so happy to see such beauty and sad that, for them, I was a source of fear.

I had accumulated almost half a bag of scallops, and I wondered how my husband had fared.

"Jeff!" I hollered, popping to the surface of the sea. "Show me what you've got so far!" We hoisted our net bags above the water, comparing catches. The daily limit per person is two gallons unshucked, or one pint of shucked scallop meat—the firm, tender, white muscle that clamps tight their shells. I had harvested at least five or six dozen, most likely my limit.

When the tide let down to dead low, there remained only the thinnest lens of clear water at the top of the water column. Grasses, fishes, scallops, and humans were compressed into just a few vertical feet. The Gulf felt cramped and itchy. Something had to go, and it was me. I climbed back into the boat. The scallops we had just harvested in less than two hours' time would require an equal amount of time to clean. We retreated upriver into the shade and organized a shucking routine.

I held a scallop in my left palm with the dark shell up and the hinge pointing away from me. I inserted a special short-bladed knife into the tiny crack at the top, detached the firm white muscle from the top shell, and handed it over to Jeff. He had the tricky part. In one smooth motion, you must slip your knife under the membrane protecting the scallop's organs. It's as if you are pulling a tight pajama shirt over a toddler's head—if you get it right, you can quickly move on. Otherwise, you've got a mess on your hands. Once you clear away the organs, you are left with a thick little muscle about the size of the end of your pinky, still attached to one shell, which you scrape into a clean bowl. By the end of the afternoon, we had produced about four modest scallop dinners to put in the freezer. Some cold winter's night, we will thaw a pint bag of these scallops to sauté with green pepper and sweet Vidalia onion from our garden. By then, the kale will be tall and green and ready to harvest and steam. We will add a side of rice and sit by fire, remembering the blazing days of summer, and scallops skittering in the grassy salt lagoons.

ONE EVENING I launched my kayak at the Indian Pass boat ramp and rode a powerful new moon tide over to the island. I dipped and pulled, tuning in to the sights and sounds of the evening. Monarch butterflies overtook me, flying faster than I could paddle. Mullet poked around in the shallow water. The loudest sound I heard was the huffing exhale of dolphins riding down the sound. On back side of the island, fronds of palms clattered in the least breeze, and I could hear even the beat of mild waves across St. Vincent Island, on the beach.

The incoming tide was just beginning to fill in around exposed clumps of oysters. I paused my paddling to watch a raccoon family foraging up to their bellies in the water. Had I walked here barefoot, the clumps of oysters (known by fisher-men as "coon" oysters) that bristle like ancient weapons would slice my feet. But the hump-backed animals stepped single file among the knife-sharp, upended mollusks as easily as if they had entered a diner.

When a raccoon digs for food in the bay bottom, she uses both front paws, grubbing like a dog in a hole. She doesn't look down. She stares into the middle distance, her eyes unhitched from focus, as if she must pour all of her senses into her paws to tease foodstuff from shell or mud. Soon enough the animals spotted my boat, and they hurried back into the island forest. Sand clung to the fur of their legs, and their belly hair dripped trails of water over the beach.

I stayed on, floating close to shore on a transparent lens of water no more than six inches deep. Intermingled among the oyster shells that had spilled from a shell mound into the bay were angular shards of very old pottery. They told me that the back side of the island was sifting into the sound: every storm event erodes away more sand, more midden, more trees. What I observed and felt was not a new human experience. Nearly the whole north shore of St. Vincent Island and much of the east shore had been inhabited over and over again for temporary camps, throughout at least four thousand years of native history and on into early historic times. People came to fish and collect shellfish, even whales, and they probably also foraged for edible plants.

Soon high tide would tuck a cool sheet of saltwater beneath the chins of the grasses and reeds, and under the feet of palms, pines, and oaks. I could not linger. There was no significant breeze, and the no-see-um gnats that staked out the island found my neck, my ears, the backs of my knees, and my scalp, and drove me away, guarding the island's secrets.

CHAPTER 5

The Passes

WEST PASS is one of four natural openings or inlets that link the inshore waters of Apalachicola Bay with the Gulf of Mexico. Together with Indian and East Passes and the Dog Island Reef, West Pass arbitrates the bay's salinity and allows mariners, dolphins, and fish to travel between the open gulf and more protected waters. A fifth opening, Sikes Cut, was dredged in 1954, severing St. George Island from Little St. George to the west. All five passages can be swift and tricky, dangerous places to be when a gale breezes up.

West Pass is the most powerful of the inlets, a virtual river. Because of its depth, up to forty or fifty feet deep in its central channel, West Pass was the most frequently used of the bay's four natural outlets by those seeking access to the commercial port of Apalachicola and its cotton trade in the 1800s.

In the 1870s a young man named George Wefing lived with his mother for five years in a house near West Pass on St. Vincent Island. He kept a journal that described the comings and goings (and mishaps) of schooners and steamships carrying cotton, lumber and other goods through West Pass. On July 31, 1879, he wrote:

> There is a small sloop [sailboat] laying to anchor in front of the house this morning.... In the evening it blew a strong breeze from the east and the little sloop began dragging her anchors and in two hours she had drug out of the bay into Gulf. About this time the wind had hauled around to the southeast the little sloop stopped dragging.
> —JOURNAL OF GEORGE WEFING

One night in March, Jeff and I and our friends Crystal and David learned the power of West Pass. We had moored a twenty-eight-foot sailboat in the pass, close to the east end of St. Vincent. Even though we were the only boaters overnighting at the time, we knew that countless square-rigged, three-masted vessels, barks, brigs, schooners, and even steamboats had anchored near this inlet over the centuries.

Just past midnight, the bright gibbous moon awoke me. An unexpected wind had risen, and it thumped our canoe in a syncopated rhythm against the hull of the sailboat.

"What do you think is going on, honey?" I reached across the narrow aisle separating our berths, to wake my husband.

"We're okay," he murmured. "Probably the tide has shifted and we are getting some waves bouncing off the shore. See if you can get back to sleep."

I registered the bump of the waves through the body of the boat, and tried to let them lull me. But we had climbed into our bunks under utterly calm conditions only a couple of hours earlier. This insistent pounding—I couldn't picture a good scenario in my mind.

"I wonder if we have run aground," I said, disentangling my legs from the bedding. "I'll go check it out."

"Tell us what you see," called Crystal from the forward cabin.

I felt for my glasses and a headlamp, pulled on a fleece jacket, and climbed up on the deck. I had to grab the cabin doorway to keep my balance—the boat was aslant, a solid clue that we had wedged against the bottom. I clicked on the flashlight and ran its tiny beam the length of the anchor line. But the rope drooped slack in the water. The anchor no longer held us safe and deep. White caps beat our starboard beam, driving the boat harder aground and heeling her further to the port side. This was not the mild breeze the weatherman had promised, nor the quiet night we'd gone to bed with. This wind blew hard enough to knock a dog's ears flat against his head.

"Uh oh, you guys," I yelled down to my companions. "The anchor has slipped! We are heeled way over. I think we are really stuck!" The other three joined me, now alert to our quandary.

"I doubt that even the high tide will be able to float us off our keel," said Jeff. "We're stuck all right."

He thought quickly. "Sue, slide down into the canoe, and David, you go next. I'll hold it steady so you won't fall in."

It was an act of faith to slip off the big boat into the rocking canoe, but adrenaline pounded me forward. Jeff passed down paddles.

"Now grab the mooring line," Jeff called to me. "Use it to pull the canoe until you feel the tug of the anchor." That was the easy part. David helped me haul the heavy anchor up into the canoe, and then we stroked like crazy into the face of the unfriendly wind, out into deeper water, where the sailboat needed to be.

The moon had almost dipped behind the island. Waves I couldn't see coming splashed my face and ran down the neck of my jacket. That same surf was hammering the boat's keel into the shallow sand bottom. David and I muscled our paddles, digging again and again into the chilly water. My shoulders burned with effort. We planted the anchor as far out as the rope allowed us, and once we'd clambered back on board, Jeff attached the anchor line to the winch on the mast.

"Okay, turn it!" hollered David, and he and Jeff reeled in the line with the winch, cranking the bow around toward the wind. This set us up perfectly for sailing off the shallows.

"I'm going to raise the main now," yelled Jeff. "If we can catch a sail full of wind, it might pull us off our keel." Crystal, David and I stood by in the cockpit as Jeff hauled the big sail into the sky.

Sure enough, as soon as the mainsail unfurled, our sloop flew straight out past the anchor, into the pitch-dark night. But at the same time, the wind blew David's brand-new kayak off the bow of the boat. Helpless, we watched that slim craft scud toward the shore of St. Vincent. Soon, it was just a shadow on the bone-white sand.

"Holy shit!" yelled David. "It's a goner!"

"We'll have to come back for it in the morning when we can actually see," Crystal said. "We've got to get a handle on this sailboat."

IN THE EARLY 1800s, ships drawing less than eight feet almost always reached the wharves at the new cotton port of Apalachicola. But vessels that drew ten feet or more water anchored a mile or two off of the Apalachicola River's mouth, off West Pass. A pilot boat would guide them through the treacherous inlet or simply unload their cargo, boat to boat. George Wefing witnessed many such passages. I imagined him watching our small drama unfold, as well:

Sunday, January 23, 1881
The day sets in with light N. wind. A three masted schooner came in today . . . the Crisie Wright. One of the pilots . . . came near being drowned when taking her up to the anchorage. He got into the white hull to bail her out and she went under with him and he swam and got an oar and kept up until they could lower a boat and pick him up. The day ends with strong N. wind and cold rain.
—JOURNAL OF GEORGE WEFING

We had a new problem on our hands. Our boat was moving briskly out the pass. There hadn't been time to haul the anchor on board, and we'd almost run out to the end of the anchor line. Jeff cut the rope and tied a boat cushion to its loose end so that we could find and retrieve our ballast again in the morning. Meanwhile, wagging like a fat tail at the sailboat's stern, the canoe had again swamped and both of our paddles had escaped into the current. Now we were sailing toward the mouth of West Pass and into the open Gulf on an outgoing tide, with neither anchor nor paddle. It wasn't full dark—there was still a bit of moon—but the islands were only visible in silhouette, and we had little idea how far we had been pulled out the pass.

"Jeff, lower the mainsail," called David. "I'll start up the motor and maybe we can get some control of our course."

Crystal was the first to notice that instead of dragging us straight out to sea, the current running through the pass was about to slam our boat against Little St. George Island, at the jaws of the inlet.

"Turn! Turn! Turn!" she screamed, as the sloop dug her keel into yet another shallows. We began to lose our humor.

"This is impossible!" Even David was running out of ideas.

Crystal and I wrapped our arms around each other for warmth.

"Should we abandon ship?" Crystal asked. The pale sands of Little St. George seemed like safer refuge than the sailboat. Neither of us had the long distance sailing experience that both of our husbands had had. Without a word, David climbed over the railing of the boat. Was he serious?

"Are you giving up on our boat?" I shouted over the driving wind. "What the heck are you doing?" I leaned over the side, watching as David began to scrabble out a ditch in the sand next to the side of the boat.

"I think if we can direct enough current to flow along the side of the boat, maybe we can float her off," he yelled.

Jeff and I caught on to David's concept. We slid into the chill water and dug like dogs with our hands. It worked. All of a sudden, the boat let go.

"Get on! Get on!" Jeff yelled, pushing me over the rail. Then he clawed his way up the side of the moving sloop. David, who had at some point stripped to his skivvies, clung to the bow. He threw one leg over the rail, then the other, clambering back on board. Crystal started up the engine. Never was there a better feeling than motoring free into the current of the pass. Somewhere behind us our anchor rested on the bottom, but we knew we wouldn't be able to look for its identifying boat cushion until morning.

It wouldn't have made us feel any better to know we weren't the first to founder in West Pass:

October 8, 1883

The day sets in with a strong gale from E. In the morning we went down on the beach and found the R. H. Porter on the beach broadside she having drug ashore during the night.

—JOURNAL OF GEORGE WEFING

Jeff and David took turns tacking with the motor, trying to stay clear of the treacherous margins of the two islands.

"We can't do this all night," David said.

Jeff rummaged through a storage locker we'd overlooked, and came up with a small auxiliary anchor. He took the sheets off the jib sail, and strung them together with every other bit of rope we could find on the boat, so we could give the diminutive anchor a ton of slack. It was four o'clock in the morning before we finally established a new anchorage far north of the mouth of West Pass, nearly up to Dry Bar. Wet, sandy, breathing hard, we groped our way below decks. Two to a sleeping bag, we finally shivered ourselves warm.

The next morning we paddled the canoe over to Tahiti Beach to collect David's kayak and the rest of our scattered gear. Then we tucked our sailboat on the bay side of St. George, in a protected curve called Pilot's Cove. No matter how pretty the paradise, no matter how calm the predicted weather, we would not risk a second night in West Pass.

WEST PASS taught me the power of an inlet between two islands, but at Indian Pass, I studied intimacy, learning all I could about what lived in those traveling, in-between waters. This, the Apalachicola River's final mouth, drains a dazzling thirteen-mile stretch of estuary referred to by locals to as "the Miles."

Indian Pass is scour-bottomed by the seesaw pull of tide and river and moon. Under the water, sand grains roll. They rub sharp corners against one another, tinkling and grinding and working at what is left of long-ago mountains. Few aquatic plants can set down roots. The pass is a living entity, sentient, embracing the bodies of millions. The microscopic young of almost every aquatic species create temporary lives in the back swirl of the tide. I could almost hear the grunts and clicks of the edge adepts that clung to the shallow pass—flounder and catfish and stingrays—for those I often saw. I wished I could hear everything—the acoustic sound-marks created by the smallest copepods and the largest tarpon. Sometimes I saw the salt Gulf water project out of itself through the bodies of mullet and tarpon and porpoise, heavy, sure, and shining. Inevitably they fell back into the water. The pass always returns to itself.

Along the lip of Indian Pass, the caucus of water and sand had built a small step-down shelf. When the tide ran clear, blue crabs and hermit crabs and little Atlantic stingrays foraged there. The rays propelled themselves by means of broad, diamond-shaped, winglike fins. Sometimes I saw dozens and dozens of rays speed-ing along the edge of the pass, pods of them, playfully darting at one another. When I went walking, my shadow frightened them and they dashed into deeper waters. In the summer and fall, I learned to raft quietly just offshore or sit very still on the beach, so I could listen to the stingrays clap their fins against the edge of the pass. It sounded like cormorants or ducks beating off the water into flight. Each animal's landward "wing-fin" emerged from the shallow water, waving like an elfin flag as the ray swam parallel to the beach, vacuuming up marine worms or tiny flounders. Every detail, every pattern of living, every sound created by pass dwell-ers that I could discern satisfied me deeply.

Once Jeff found a stingray jaw in a saltmarsh. It took us a while to figure out what it was. The flat sturdy bone was shaped like two sides of a triangle, similar to a denture plate, but with fused teeth. As a ray prowls along the bottom, it stirs up the sand and fer-rets out soft-bodied invertebrates, crushing what it captures with this jaw. One exceptionally clear morning, I watched a ray plow through the sand along the pass. Displaced grit drifted back into his eyes, and he blinked in long slow fleshy flickers to clear his sight.

Think of stingrays as pancake versions of a shark, an animal perfectly designed for life on the bottom of the sea. Their eyes and their breathing spiracles protrude from the tops of their heads. Scientists describe them as dorsally compressed, which means they can watch for danger from above while they feed on what they excavate beneath them in the sand. Stingrays have lived long enough in our oceans to have a claim on this place. They predate humans on the planet by 150 million years. I have come to admire them dearly.

A ray will not strike a human with the stinger under its tail unless it is pinned down and feels threatened for its life. All of us who enter this warm salt water have been taught the tactically effective "stingray shuffle." Instead of wading through the water as if you were stepping along the ground, the idea is to keep your feet connected to the sand. Then, if you inadvertently come within range of a ray, the commotion will scare the shy but well-defended animal out of your path. To my mind, rays are tiny underwater angels, innocent of any ill intent.

I AM CERTAIN that birds ride Indian Pass for pleasure. Many times I have watched a single pied-billed grebe, a pod of pelicans, a common loon, or a flock of gulls or mergansers catch a swift lift from the sound to the Gulf, not fishing, not doing anything at all except resting on the outbound flow.

We liked to do that, too. Over the years, our family acquired an odd fleet of boats. The Christmas our boys turned ten we bought them each an eight-foot Swifty kayak, one white and one red. Jeff preferred a lime-green sit atop designed to ride the surf. An old Mohawk canoe stored upside down in the front yard added to our capacity when boatless friends or relatives joined in an outing. Then there was a cumbersome, twenty-five-year-old midnight blue sea kayak, the first I ever bought for myself. It was so heavy that it mostly collected pollen and oak leaves under a heavy azalea hedge in the back corner of our yard where a couple of brown thrashers nested each spring. We loaned all of these boats to our friend Irwin, a black-bearded, banana-powered angel of a man who ran a simple summer camp to get kids out in nature. We liked knowing our flotilla took children deep into the rivers and swamps, far from video games, even just for a day, or a week.

I didn't share my personal favorite with Irwin's gang, because it had a cranky rudder and easily wounded flippers. This short, blunt-tipped Hobie wasn't built for speed, but its adaptations allowed me to use the strong muscles of my thighs to get where I wanted to go. An eight-pound foot pedal drive dropped into a slot in the belly of the kayak, and with these alternating pedals I could stroke through the water as if I rode a bicycle on land. The pedals connected to a pair of flexible underwater fins, and they worked much like a penguin's flippers to propel the kayak through the water. The boat had a decently comfortable clip-in seat, so I could lean into my back for more leverage. Imagine the position of a recumbent bicycle: alternating steps on pedals in the cockpit caused two underwater fins to flex, sweeping the boat forward. Although the flippers sliced silently through the water, waves on the surface thrummed against the Hobie's broad prow. The rudder was controlled by a line that ran through the interior of the boat to a lever I manipulated with my left hand. It strained and creaked as I adjusted my course over the water. My right hand was free to grab a paddle if I needed to, or hold binoculars up to my eyes. It took a bit of coordination, but it was worth it. My kayak was not useful on a lime-rock-bottom river like the Suwannee, nor along the sunny corridors of the Wacissa or the Wakulla, where lengths of underwater grasses fouled the rudder and flippers. Shallow ledges and oyster reefs tripped her up, too.

What she was perfect for was Indian Pass. I could match Jeff paddling his sit atop against a stiff breeze or a running tide, because all my effort was out of the wind, under the water's surface. My kayak gave me freedom to explore these fast-moving waters alone, anytime I wanted. And when I chose to stop paddling or pedaling, I was carried at the pace of a much larger body. My risings and fallings were the Gulf's, my pitch and my roll determined by the water and the wind.

Using a motor to push your boat and your body through the water is fast and convenient, but it lands you with a jolt at your destination. There is a surrealism to gas-powered travel that can make me feel "not there," not fully present. I don't believe I appreciate the journey as much. Whereas when I traveled by kayak, after all that salt and struggle and aching shoulders, the wind burn, the long sweat, then the moment of sliding the hull of the boat against the beach is a deep release stamped on my senses. Not just an "oh, we're there" kind of thing, not like that at all.

WHEN THE TIDE TURNS on a calm day, salt water bunches into the pass, sagging in fine floury wrinkles. It resembles a very old person's skin. The surface of the water is also the integument of dolphins, air-breathing mammals necessarily contiguous with both elements. I love to watch them slip the pass and surge whole-bodied into the sky. In winter when a front moves through and the wind swings around to the north, the dolphins seem to relish the slap of cold air as they leap and leap again, straight into the western-born wind.

I always hoped that dolphins would claim kinship with me and my boat since I was flipper driven, not gas powered. But dolphins are wired for speed and turbulent play, and the Hobie and I were too slow and uninteresting to hold their attention for long. Most of our close encounters were simple interceptions—I was in the path of their travel or in the vicinity of the fish they were seeking. Still, when I paddled on the pass, I always watched for the dolphins, alert for a chance to connect.

One evening as I sat on the porch of our rented house, I noticed a dozen dolphins working the pass together, their bodies lifting and sinking in and out of the water, as if they revolved on a wheel. The water was smooth and pink, and their bodies glinted like nickel in the angling set of the sun. One animal vaulted high, its mouth stretched into a fixed grin. I ran down the steps, slid my kayak into the water, and paddled into their path.

Across the pass on the point of the island, pelicans dozed, brown and rounded like soft mammals. Their bills were tucked along their backs, but they kept one eye open, watching for trouble. One bird yawned and aimed its pouched bill vertically into the air. Younger pelicans bathed at the edge, lifting water overhead and beating it over their backs, then paddling ashore to oil and organize their feathers.

I balanced my boat in the confusion of current just off the point, moving neither in nor out. The stink of bird guano filled my nostrils. Olfactory overload made me feel seasick and vulnerable. Suddenly I was surrounded by fins and backs, a tail, a face with one bright black eye. The dolphins had gathered up to check me out. They swam in pairs and threes, narrow fins so close, I figured they must be pressed skin to skin under the water. I could hear their sharp explosive out breaths, even felt the soft spray of mist forced from their blowholes. I, the watcher, was being observed. Now things were more equal. I was keenly aware of their power and of my precarious balance on the little boat I paddled. The dolphins could have easily nudged me right over into the outgoing tide if they chose. It's a good thing to know where you stand. It's a good thing to understand that fear is integral to awe. When the dolphins moved out into the Gulf, the pass felt vastly empty.

CHAPTER 6

Upland *Where the Beach Used to Be*

ON HER KNEES, Dr. Jean Huffman sifted through the frost-faded grasses all the way down to scalp of the land. It was as if she parted the hair of a beloved child, loosening a tangle or preparing to weave a braid. But what her long fingers sought were the crowns of the scarcest of plants.

"I believe I am motivated by beauty," said Jean, the manager of the St. Joseph Bay State Buffer preserve and an expert on fire and its effects on the landscape. She was searching for the rootstock of a yellow aster named Chapman's crownbeard, a plant whose presence would confirm that we were in just the right place to find plants even more rare. But that late December day, many of the endangered wildflowers lay dormant. Not until the weather warmed would they offer their intricate designs and vibrant color to the sky. We would have to content ourselves with what evidence we could find.

How would the land cover be different on St. Vincent (or St. George, or Dog) if the islands were able to stay above sea level and survive another ten centuries? Those barrier islands are young and relatively simple in plant composition. I had come to this preserve to compare its much, much older system of dune ridges and swales—and magnificent diversity of plants—with those off-shore on St. Vincent Island. Even though the sea hadn't touched the preserve in millennia, it was so near the coast I could hear waves breaking at the outlet of Money Bayou through the pines. The satellite images for the two landscapes—island refuge and inland preserve—appear similar, but the coast-parallel ridges that score this preserve—only five miles as the gull flies, across the narrow neck of land that divides Indian Pass and the town of Port

St. Joe—have recently been aged at well over a hundred thousand years. The oldest ridge on St. Vincent is less than four thousand years old. That island is a mere baby compared to St. Joe's set of venerable coastlines.

"AS ON ST. VINCENT, old dune ridges and the previous shorelines completely determined the plant communities you'll find on this preserve," Jean said. "We've got seven dune ridges between Money Bayou and the Gulf. The rarest plants are found in the swales between the most ancient ridges, and the number of endangered plants is bumped up by certain little plants that abound there. Mostly they grow in what botanists call basal rosettes."

Jean uncovered a rough bouquet of small leaves. To my eye, the winter-disguised plant was unremarkable. This was definitely one of the times when a picture is worth any number of words. I hope as you read this, you will look up an image of Chapman's crownbeard in a field guide or on your computer. It is so rare, you may otherwise.never see it. In bud, this daisy relative is composed of a cluster of butter yellow trumpets, each lunging straight toward the sun.

Unique as it is, the crownbeard is only one of 427 different plant species that have been found on Buffer Preserve lands. An astounding 21 are listed as threatened or endangered. Their names reflect their beauty: white-birds-in-a-nest, Godfrey's golden aster, green spider-lily, violet-flower butterwort, to name just a few.

"None of our endangered plants occur on the barrier islands," said Jean. "Nor do they grow here on the youngest of our dune ridges." The land has to settle and prepare a long, long time to grow the rarest of the rare.

WE BUMPED ALONG Treasure Road in Jean's ATV. She navigated the landscape with the instincts of someone moving about her own familiar neighborhood. Just a few unpaved roads have been plowed atop the ancient linear dunes in this preserve; one hundred millennia of weathering have flattened the once-upon-a-time beach ridges to stripes of droughty sand. Jean cut the wheel sharply, taking us off the side of the road to park. We struck out on foot through flatwoods punctuated by sparse and stunted pines. Most of the rare plants grew in a meandering zone of habitat invisible from the rough sand road, so we waded downhill through grasses as high as our thighs, Jean in the lead, slim and long limbed as a great blue heron. Her field garb included badly beaten tennis shoes, faded jeans, and a long-sleeved denim shirt.

"This place has elevation!" called Jean, over her shoulder. "Oh yeah, it really does!" She wanted to make sure I noticed the subtle slope of the land as we skirted around scrub oak, gallberry, and fetterbush and stepped over the snaky trunks of saw palmetto (even the names of these flatwoods plants seem to slow a visitor's passage). Blackened claws of the burnt shrubs striped my khaki pants charcoal.

Very few pine or cypress trees on this preserve are sufficiently tall enough to offer shade. Most are less than fifty years old. Settlers of European origin drained the resin from the original old-growth longleaf pines in the early 1900s, then logged it completely in the 1930s. People captured and ate gopher tortoises until none remained and used the land for open-range grazing of cattle and hogs. Finally, many of the stumps of the longleaf pine (some aged at more than five hundred years old) were levered out of the ground and sold for fat lighter.

"When there was nothing left to take," said Jean as we approached the cypress wetland at the bottom of the slope, "the land was essentially abandoned until the state bought it and pieced it together into a preserve in the 1990s, mostly to protect the water quality of St. Joe Bay from development.

"This is a little five-thousand-acre preserve. It's not the original landscape, because of canopy variations, and we should be connected to larger chunks of wild land for big animals like bears to roam. But it's better than anywhere else around here."

And as the name of the main sand road—Treasure—implies, the preserve still harbors inestimable value. Although everything else was taken, the groundcover is still intact.

Jean turned back to the path we had just negotiated. "Up there are the pine flatwoods," she said with a wide sweep of her arm. "See how they intergrade down into the cypress wetlands ahead?" The rare plants we sought hid beneath the grasses in a swath of habitat between the pine flatwoods and the wetland swales.

"And here we are," she announced. "Right in the red hot zone!"

The narrow belt of wet savanna where most of the rare plants grow is only about ten to twenty feet wide, irregular, following the contours of the wetland, covered by thick clumps of fine grasses. The ground squished under my feet as I squatted beside Jean on the ground. We raked through the dead grasses with our hands and uncovered a clutch of tiny red sundew leaves, some yellow-green butterworts, and a patch of parrot pitcher plants, all hugged close to the ground, waiting for the weather to warm.

Jean sat back on her heels, pulled off her tall straw hat, and ran her fingers through her short, straight hair, the same soft blonde as wiregrass. Her hazel eyes burned. "Most people have heard of pitcher plants, but actually, many of our rare species are carnivorous," she said. "There are so many reasons to find them fascinating."

SUDDENLY I REMEMBERED a long-ago dream; I hadn't understood it at the time. The bottoms of my feet were itching, as if I had blisters from an allergic reaction. When I reached down to scratch the sole of my right foot, I found a luxuriant growth of pitcher plants rooted into my skin. Completely startled, I began to pull out hanks of the fleshy plants. But I stopped myself, realizing that they profoundly interconnected me with the ground. By growing into my skin, the plants insisted that I pay attention to my—our—essential relationship with Earth.

Jean was off on her own train of thought.

"Outside of the Buffer Preserve, this ecosystem and its history—the result of thousands of years of evolution—is so gone," she said. "People clear it, right and left; what grows here naturally doesn't seem to mean a thing to them. And then it is lost to us forever. I could drive you to some land in Port St. Joe where bulldozers are scraping away Chapman's rhododendrons for a development this very minute. They will never come back."

Chapman's rhododendrons, one of the preserve's signature plants, are related to the cultivated azaleas common to every southern garden, but they grow in a dry and fire-dependent habitat. I thought of the times I had stumbled upon those beauties while surveying for red-cockaded woodpeckers in Florida's national forests and how, in April, the plants extended stiff stalks of extravagant rose-pink flowers high in the air. They are a sight to behold and a scent to deeply inhale.

In the span of a human life, Chapman's rhododendrons and their habitat have been almost entirely obliterated. The Buffer Preserve is the only public land that protects this federally endangered species.

"That is why I've been so committed to tending and restoring this place," Jean said. During her eight years as preserve manager, Jean had returned a more natural fire regime and water flow to this five-thousand-acre landscape.

"We have done a lot of invisible restoration, like filling in this plow line," she said, pointing at what had once been a ditch that divided the cypress wetland from the drier pine woods upslope. "So many of the grassy edges between cypress wetlands and uplands were ditched to exclude fire from the wetlands. Draining the land made it easier for people to log, then graze cattle and hogs. But that is a problem, because 90 percent of our rare plants live in those zones."

In Florida, a land manager needs to tease out, understand, and then restore how water moves across the land. At the same time, she must reintroduce controlled fire to the landscape.

"This was all grown up with unbelievably impenetrable titi shrubs when I came on as manager here eight years ago," Jean said. "There hadn't been any fire in here for some forty or fifty years. Without those fires the landscape had lost its definitions and all its subtle transitions. The plant communities had become blurred. But when you bring back fire and burn on a regular basis, the habitats are defined as clearly as can be," she continued.

The landscape around us corroborated Jean's story. Fire-scarred trunks of the pines spoke of the recent passage of flames, and the bones of overgrown shrubs pointed ebony fingers to the sky.

"Restoration is the most rewarding part of my job. I am completely motivated by maintaining the diversity in this herbaceous ground cover, so I've been concentrating on restoring these wet savanna zones and the rare plants that live in them."

As we crouched next to the precious swath of wildflowers, Jean told me more of what she had learned in her years managing the preserve. "We now know that to restore these little grassy zones, we have to burn during the growing season. Fire synchronizes the blooming of so many flowers, including asters, liatris, and carphephorus. Normally these areas would have burned very frequently, lit by summer lightning storms.

"If you don't burn in the summer, titi, pines, and other woody species encroach in the rare plant zone. Our first burn reduced the overgrown titi to shrub skeletons. And after repeated fires, the woody plants had been burned back to a more natural occurrence pattern, liberating all these wildflowers, giving them room to thrive and bloom.

"I go in the field all the time with people, even land managers, who simply: Don't. Know. Plants. Trees, shrubs, and weeds, that's basically all they see.

"But to me," she said, her voice both intense and confiding. "The ground cover is what it's about. Trees are easy.

"Sometimes another land manager will say to me, 'Well, you've got grasses. Look at all this broom sedge. Aren't you happy?'

"I can hardly answer that question without exploding," she continued, with a humorless laugh. "No, I'm not satisfied with that. I would have no reason to be happy if the result of my work were a field of broom sedge.

"The land manager might continue the conversation and say to me: 'But broom sedge is a fine fuel, it's great for carrying the fire.'

"'Think about it,'" I'll ask them. "'What is the purpose of carrying fire? It is to maintain the natural diversity of the land, not just grow a field of one kind of grass!'

"Do you see what I'm up against?" she asked me, throwing her hands up in the air. "Do you know what I mean?"

I BELIEVED I DID. I thought about a recent morning riding my bike along the off-road Munson Hills trail close to my home in Tallahassee. Three miles out, I scraped the trunk of a turkey oak tree with my bicycle, folding my metal derailleur into an impotent knot.

I knew that it would be a long schlep on foot, pushing my bike back to the road. But I also knew I would be happy, moving more slowly. I could listen to the calls of Bachman's sparrows and red-cockaded woodpeckers. I could look down at the mosaic of plants along the trail and take time to notice the wind that foretold a tropical storm.

This pine woods, called Munson Hills (part of the Apalachicola National Forest), is well managed with prescribed, frequent fires. As I made my way, I observed how powdery blue spears of broom sedge arrowed from the forest floor in the wake of a recent burn. It wasn't growing in monocultural fields, as it might if the ground cover and seed banks had been scraped away by bulldozers, or if fire was suppressed or unnaturally forced to the winter months. Here, broom sedge sprouted in patches the size of my arms encircled, between regrowing runner oak and single pink meadow beauties and spreading pawpaw plants and wiregrass, lilting in the wind. Broom sedge is an honorable member of the pine flatwoods community, but only when it shares the spaces, pruned by the natural season of fire. Embedded in such diversity, the Bachman's sparrow can find a varied diet of seed and insect, and so can the bluebird and the fox squirrel and the gopher tortoise. When fire is suppressed to serve human convenience, the land is forced into monoculture, offending and starving its potential range of biodiversity.

AS THE SUN SET, we headed back to Jean's ATV. "Isn't it odd?" she mused. "Anything people have built, like a lighthouse or a building, is thrilling to visitors. Even if the structure is only a hundred years old, you can raise mountains of money and get tons of volunteer hours. People appreciate that St. Joseph Bay State Buffer Preserve harbors twenty known archaeological and historical sites, dating from prehistoric times through the present. But endangered plants? Sometimes I'll lead a tour group of several dozen folks out here, and only one or two will want to get off the cart and walk out with me to look at these incredible species. For most visitors, this landscape—a hundred thousand years in the making—simply doesn't register.

"To me, this preserve is like a little museum, part art, part history, of what has been evolving here so very long before we humans arrived. When I walk through the seasons on this land, after eight years of restoration work, it's always a surprise, it's always new and it's always beautiful, so much fun to watch. Every week there is something new blooming, all these little treasures."

I scanned the landscape that had appeared so unremarkable to me just a few hours before. The half-grown longleaf pines, finely needling the sky, looked like they were in it for the long haul. Sun slanted gold on the wiregrass flowers. I knew I'd want to come back.

PART 2   *Territory*

We live in a world mapped by Western law and philosophy, and that is how we determine what and how places and beings are "owned." Earlier peoples and other forms of nature besides the human lived—and live—in this place so much more seamlessly than we do. By watching how wild birds define territory, and how the first Floridians knew and claimed their places here, we may learn to distinguish between what we want and what we need. Looking through their eyes, or trying to, I have begun to understand how this landscape was once shared, then stolen, and may again be used in common.

CHAPTER 7

The First People

FOR AS LONG AS these islands have existed, people navigated the shellfish-studded lagoons and bays in search of food. They belonged to a host of aboriginal groups—the Apalachicoli (who gave their name to the river), the Chisca, the Sawokli, the Chatot, the Amacano, the Chine, and the Pacara—remnants of unnamed prehistoric ancestors. Based on the artifacts they left behind, these peoples have been classified by archaeologists into the Archaic, Norwood, Deptford, Weedon Island, Santa Rosa–Swift Creek, and Fort Walton cultures. All told, the tenure of the original Floridians familiar with this ground dates back more than twelve thousand years on the mainland, four thousand years on the islands—many hundreds of generations. In contrast, a modern family descended from the earliest European settlers of North Florida in the late 1800s may claim five or six generations living here, at most.

The Amacano were first mentioned in the late 1620s as a people who lived along the coast south and southeast of the Apalachee at that time. When the Amacano next appear in Spanish accounts in 1674, they were living with two other peoples identified as Chine and Pacaro in a village ten to eleven leagues distant from the Apalachee in a southerly direction, possibly near modern Spring Creek opposite Piney Island. The Chine were distinguished in the eyes of the Spaniards as pilots with experience traveling by canoe from St. Mark's to the place of Pensacola. The Pacara were faceless to the Spaniards, appearing only a few times in passing reference; nothing was written identifying individuals, activities, or customs.

For the first people on this landscape, the coastal terrain was a commons, and movement was on foot. Before the introduction of agriculture, people shifted between favorite productive locations, harvesting seeds, nuts, and fruit during the spring and fall; hunting during the winter; and fishing whenever there was something to catch.

"Landholding as an end in itself is unnecessary when human numbers are small and nature is a shared 'storehouse,'" wrote Paul Shepard in *Coming Home to the Pleistocene*. "Primal peoples do not own land and evince little absolute territoriality."

Florida archaeologists concur and suggest that when villages or camps grew too large to be supported easily from local resources, several households might "bud off" and found a new village close by. People living almost entirely from wild foods could not—and knew not—to overcollect.

The meander of a river, the shine of an island, the drop of a scarp, the sparkle of a large spring—these were territorial markers, signposts of home—during the first twelve thousand years of human tenure here. How much different your perspective of a place would be if you knew you lived between an island and the mainland, or between two rivers that you must ford if you wished to leave home. You are here on this side of the water, and through the physical effort of your own body paddling a hollowed-out cypress canoe or even swimming, you cross over and arrive on the opposite shore. Your body participates in the definition of its place.

But no words, no songs, no stories remain to describe these original peoples' four-thousand-year relationship with what we think of as "our coast." Nothing remains of their languages. We know very little about how they defined their territories or thought about the place that they lived.

What we have are accounts written by the first Europeans who came to Florida: fortune hunters, pirates, and missionaries. The European conquistadors didn't know nor care to learn the languages and customs of the people they encountered. But the Spanish were often accompanied by Catholic priests who strung missions from St. Augustine to Pensacola, and their presence probably had much to do with the practice of naming the bays, capes, and islands after the Catholic saint upon whose feast day a particular landform was "discovered." According to historian G. M. West, there is no other stretch of North American shoreline with so many place names derived from Christian saints as this Gulf Coast between St. Marks on the east and Santa Rosa on the west (including St. George, St. Teresa, St. James, St. Vincent, San Blas, St. Joseph, and St. Andrew). You could say that in no other area has local identity been so erased by the icons of another continent's religion.

The colonizers' journals and letters largely reflect their own agendas and tell us almost nothing about the tribes they robbed or converted, and eventually displaced. Here is a tantalizing fragment:

"In the estuary . . . there are many oysters; judging by the tumble-down *bohios*, or fishermen's huts, on the banks," wrote Carlos de Siguenza y Gongora about Pensacola Bay when he visited there in the spring of 1693 in the company of Admiral Pez. "It is doubtless much frequented by the Indians in the summertime, which is the season when they come down to their fisheries on the seacoast after preparing their inland cornfields."

Seventy-five years later, you can read the briefest reference to a coastal family, although the anecdote actually focuses on Pierre Viaud, a Frenchman shipwrecked on Dog or St. George Island. Viaud wandered for months, starving, until he was eventually rescued. During his enforced island stay, he encountered an Indian named Antonio and his mother, wife, sister, and nephew. He observed that the family resided in a hut and that they fished, hunted, and moved slowly across the landscape. That's all we know of them.

From such wisps of information, we can assume that the area's early natives moved between temporary fishing camps on the coast and a more permanent place farther inland, utilizing the abundant natural resources as the seasons delivered them. What we can never fully understand is the powerful, very particular sense of identity of the original peoples, including how they knew themselves to belong to a very specific, bounded space. This is a great loss—historically, culturally, and spiritually—for from these people we could have learned how to live in reciprocity with the land that sustains us. How many of us know that our place (wherever that is) makes us who we are?

Here is how it was, according to an account of the Pez expedition in 1693 that surprised two small parties of unidentified Indians along an inlet or stream near Pensacola Bay while they were preparing a midday meal. The Indians fled, leaving behind a detailed scene of all that they had had, and all that was taken from them.

In the campsites, the Spaniards noted "a fire lit and a poorly made earthen pan placed by it with some tastelessly stewed buffalo lungs"; reed baskets that contained maize and pumpkin seeds; a variety of pemmican; baskets containing "fibrous and sweet" lily or ginger roots; numerous pots and pans with gourd dippers and ladles of buffalo horn; ten to twelve buffalo hides and "uncured pelts of martens, foxes, otters, and many deer."

They also found quantities of buffalo hair, some in balls and some on distaffs; little buckskin bags filled with the hair of beaver, soft white feathers, wooden combs, leather shoes, claws of birds and animals, and "a thousand other small objects"; earthen pigments for body painting; "feather headdresses placed for safekeeping between carefully tied pieces of tree bark, made from feathers of turkeys, cardinals and various other birds."

And there were huts fashioned with sloping roofs covered with "bark stripped from pine trees with considerable skill" to keep each piece intact; a medium-sized fishing craft with "an indefinite number of bows and arrows"; tattered blue cloth of Spanish manufacture; hanging baskets of little shells of mother-of-pearl, fish scales, animal bones, and tufts of hair.

The Indians had created lives from the place they lived, and they knew they belonged there in a way that only indigenous people truly can. They lived consciously within an exquisite balance that included human beings. To become animal, not have that division—that's why they wore the skins in ceremony. They were comprised directly and intimately, cell by cell, of the generosity of land and sea.

All this was taken from them.

TO FIND our own sense of place, what we have are our own bodies of experience. When the children were young, we spent many weekends at the coast. At the tail end of one such day, I watched over the boys as Jeff cranked our boat onto its trailer at the Lanark boat ramp. Water streamed off the hull and the motor. We had spent the warm autumn day on Dog Island, swimming and playing in the Gulf. Our boys filled buckets with seawater and ran along the edge of the wavelets with small dip nets, collecting blue crabs, jellyfish, and hermits. Mullet glided through the green shallows, pursued by Jeff and his cast net. The boys rescued a cannonball jellyfish from the sand where it had been stranded by the outgoing tide. We took turns reaching into a plastic bucket filled with saltwater, cupping the smooth body of the jelly in our hands, like a baby's head, bald and moist and vulnerable. We admired the wee fish that lived up under the animal's translucent mantle. Watching those fishlets glean bits of food, that too was a wonderful part of the day. And so was the release of that jellyfish community back into its sea.

Now it was time to go home.

"Mom, look, the prickly pears are ripe!" called David. "Can't we stay a little bit longer?" With his stepbrother, Patrick, my son had waded into the weeds between the ramp and the road. The boys were bronzed and lean, and their hair was stiff with salt. They didn't want the outdoor day to end.

The juicy magenta fruits of the prickly pear cactus were tricky to harvest, but we knew how. Before you pluck the figlike fruit, you must scrape off the tufts of needle-fine spines with a knife or a shell. Otherwise, you'll end up with a painful cluster of hairlike splinters in your fingers and tongue. The boys and I could have filled a bucket with prickly pear fruit, but Jeff was ready to get on the road.

"Gotta go now, guys," I said. Monday's school and work obligations in town loomed like thunder clouds. We had to telescope time at the coast into weekend days, because our home was forty miles north and west across the Ochlockonee River.

As I climbed into the front seat of the car, I imagined the life of a long-ago coastal family, similar to ours. I shaded my eyes with my hand and stared back at the island across the sun-spangled water. I am certain how we just spent our day exactly resembles what men and women and children did in this place for thousands of years. The women and the youngest gathering—so many things!—prickly pears, blueberries, blackberries, acorns, hickory nuts, and crabs. The women weaving nets from the fiber of palm so their men could seine the spawning mullet and the shrimp. The women coiling clay into pots, tempering them with Spanish moss, and firing them to hardness, to contain and cook their food. And like my family, back and forth the people traveled, mainland to island, and even inland, following the readiness of the food. But never so quickly as we do today.

BEGINNING WITH the prowl of Spanish pirates along the coastline of North America in the early sixteenth century, the common terrain of Florida's peoples transformed into lawlessly exploited, foreign-held territories. One after another, the Spanish, the French, and the British claimed Florida, seizing all they could carry off and ship back to Europe. Each of the colonizing countries took a turn operating under what Barry Lopez calls "the assumption of an imperial right conferred by God, sanctioned by the state, and enforced by a militia, the assumption of unquestioned superiority over a resident people." In the end, Spain ceded Florida to the United States in 1819.

Some of the native people tried to hide and survive the repeated invasions on one or another of the barrier islands. In a letter penned on July 8, 1704, a Spanish deputy described skirmishes with English attackers and talked about the likely fate of the native Indians living in Spanish missions. He wrote that "in the matter of going to the Presidio, they neither wish that, for they would have the same risk should the English surround the fort, and they care not but to go to the woods or to the isles of the sea, each one to where God will aid. This is a decision with which they have replied to me."

He continued: "The priests also say they do not wish to remain here, that they would go to the isles, they know not where, and that already they have written to their prelate."

Even greater numbers of Florida's first peoples were killed by a cavalcade of fatal viruses unleashed by the Europeans. A holocaust was the result. "In the annals of human history," writes Charles C. Mann in *1493: Uncovering the New World Columbus Created*, "there is no comparable demographic catastrophe." Except for handfuls of Indians who fled the state, tribes indigenous to the Panhandle and its coast were largely exterminated by the mid-eighteenth century. Today, only a few people living in Louisiana can trace their ancestry to Florida's indigenous population.

This land lay empty for nearly two hundred years until other American Indians—the Creeks and the Seminoles from Georgia and Alabama—began to reinfuse the Panhandle lands vacated by disease and warfare. Through trade with the Creeks, European merchants and trading houses began to siphon off the natural resources of the region. The English firm of John Forbes and Company established a monopoly over the Creek trade in the late 1800s and reaped high profits from furs procured for them by the Indians. In just one year (1797), Forbes received sixty thousand pounds of deer, raccoon, fox, otter, and wildcat skins into their Pensacola warehouse for shipping. What the Indians wanted in return were manufactured goods, including silk, velveteen, cotton, and wool cloth. Most of all, they wished to acquire metal products, including padlocks, knives, needles, axes, bullets, and other arms.

I try to imagine the two peoples—European trader and Florida Indian—coming together in a rough wooden trade house to exchange desire. For the European, these transactions had to do with financial gain. At the time, the Europeans were not interested in the land itself, except that they understood that "the extension of the fur trade depends entirely upon the Indians being undisturbed in the possession of their hunting grounds, and that all colonizing does in its nature, and must in its consequence, operate to the detriment of that branch of commerce. . . . Let the savages enjoy their desert in quiet. Were they driven from the forests the peltry [fur]-trade would decrease."

The Indian wanted to replace his whelk hoe for a tool with a metal edge. Such an implement would enable him to slice through roots and soil with less backbreaking effort, as he prepared the ground to plant corn and squash. And he needed iron ax blades to sever the young sweet gum trees that were springing up at the edges of his fields. And he wanted woven fabric because he had watched his wife rub a length of cotton between her fingers. How much easier it would be to stitch than a deerskin, she said, and he knew that was true.

So what would the family offer up in trade? The skins of the animals of the forest.

To buy the goods his family needed and the things they had learned to desire, the Indian would have to kill and skin many more forest-dwelling furbearers than ever before.

I imagine him wondering, How many people must there be across the sea, to warm themselves under all these skins? The prayers he was taught—to thank the animal for its life so that his people might eat and stay warm—no longer seemed relevant. The worth of the lives of the twenty-nine deer this man had so recently stalked, shot, skinned, and cured were to be applied to the tools, ammunition, cloth, spices, and a bit of whiskey that the trader kept in a keg behind the counter. But they wouldn't be enough. And the glossy-furred otters that used to muscle and loop through the blackwater creeks had retreated far upriver, pressed by overhunting. Foxes appeared only infrequently now, and there were no more black bears for miles. The hunter would have to go farther inland to procure more—and smaller—prey.

I THOUGHT about this as I walked on a forest trail south of Tallahassee. Before I ever saw it, I heard a distinctive scrabbling on tree bark, and I knew I was close to one of my favorite animals, a fox squirrel. I caught a glimpse of her as she bounded to a small pine and shuffled about eight feet up the trunk. Not safe enough. She shimmied back down as if the tree were a fire station pole and made for a full-grown tree yards away through the wiregrass. Up, up, up: with her forearms and her sharp nails, she gripped the tree in a series of ascending, widespread hugs. Flakes of bark chipped off and flew into the air over my head. The animal peered around at me as she climbed. Secretive and cryptic, the fox squirrel clung to the far side of the pine, nearly at the top. I guessed that she would stay in this tree now, so I lay down on the sandy trail with my binoculars to watch. I spotted a small fluff of her fur, colored fog and fawn, through the tree branches. She didn't move, so I rolled over and eased myself around the column of tree. Now I could see the whole of the squirrel plastered against the pine, as flat as a thick-furred animal could make herself be. Her eyes were fixed and glassy, her forelimbs and her mottled paws gripped the tree. There was a single fawn spot on her black foot. She assumed I could not see her, so she did not flee.

I thought, "Exactly now is when the Indian would let his arrow fly."

THE CREEKS could not keep pace with what they owed to the English trading firm. Between 1804 and 1811, they were persuaded to pay off their substantial debts by granting three tracts of land to the company—an unimaginable million and a half acres, including all the offshore islands from the mouth of the Wakulla River to the mouth of the Apalachicola, and far north into the interior of the Panhandle. This transaction, called the Forbes Purchase, was the pipeline for all subsequent property ownership in North Florida as we know it today. Beginning in the mid-1820s, there was a general survey of public lands conducted in Florida to designate township, range, and section boundaries. And then, one after another, the islands fell into private hands: St. Vincent Island was sold to Robert Floyd in 1858; Dog Island to private individuals in 1860; Little St. George to Thomas Orman in 1861; and St. George Island to George Sinclair in 1881.

The original names, the wisdom and culture, the history and languages of many centuries of vibrant peoples native to our coast have vanished forever. With the genocide of the original peoples, we forfeited a profound opportunity to understand our landscape. We lost twelve thousand years of story on this land, story that once made sense of the islands and the forest, how they grow and what they support, how we in turn must live. How does such poverty of heritage relate to attachment and stewardship of our coast? Our European forebears viewed this continent as a place to transcend and were incapable of allowing themselves to be touched by the continent as a presence of the divine. Because we do not know the story we have emerged from, we do not understand what our culture has done and is doing to the lives already here. Perhaps this is why whatever evidence of deep time we find can be so powerful.

ONE DAY I stood at the edge of the clear salt water and noticed fragments of ancient pottery layered among the oyster shells that paved the island's transition into the bay. With a length of silvery cedar, I raked a few of the jigsawed clay fragments onto the shore so I could study their patterns. One was a decoratively edged, palm-sized piece of pottery, swelled wide, as if it encircled the trunk of a sapling pine. Perhaps it was once part of a shallow bowl used to store berries, seeds, or even a wild edible grain. I could see that the artist had shredded fiber from a cabbage palm just like one behind me, woven it into netting, and pressed it into the clay. Other designs were incised, perhaps with the fine, sharp tip of black needle rush: half-moon brackets, dots and dashes, and two circles with single dots in the center. It resembled a Morse code of sorts, written thousands of years ago in a language I would never understand.

I rotated the piece lengthwise. Suddenly I saw what the artist so obviously intended: the face of a fish. Its eyes were perfectly round and bulging, punctuated by deep pinpoint pupils. I knew this kind of fish, and I knew its suffering expression.

Sailtop cats are one of the commonest fish we catch in these island passes. One April morning, I hooked an especially large individual in the mouth of Big Bayou. It was as if a great weight had struck my line, pulling our boat into deeper water. My reel creaked and strained as I hauled the heavy animal on board. I had hoped for something more edible, but at least it would be easy to release—only its lip was snagged on my fluorescent-headed lure. Steering clear of the cat's defensive spines, I twisted the hook away with pliers. The fish grunted in pain, and Jeff quickly nudged it back overboard with the handle of our landing net. But before it splashed away, I noted that the fish's lips were downturned just like the one etched onto the piece of pottery I'd found. The shape of the catfish's mouth is an artifact of its physiognomy, yes, but also I recognized, as did the creator of this pottery, the despond of one about to be dinner. The Indian who fashioned and etched this clay vessel speaks to me over the centuries, of both the catch and the acknowledgment of an animal's pain.

Through the design of her pottery, the language of her art, and my eyes, the long-ago Indian woman and I reach across time. Even though for her race of people, history has ended, I realize that my body and my hands are linked directly to those who baited hooks, bore children, and paddled canoes thousands of years before this life I live.

CHAPTER 8

Beach Badges

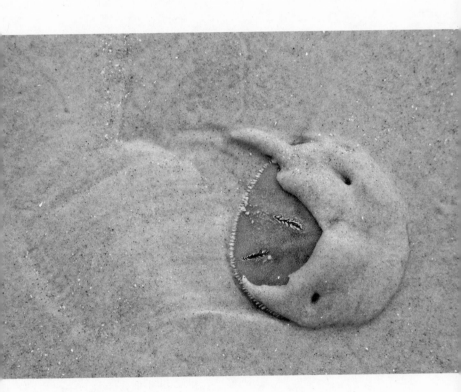

WHEN YOU ARE BORN into a system of thought, you have only that perspective to tell you what is right or wrong. But an unjust system can feel amiss, even early in life, and it was as a young child that I began to chafe at the fact that the Jersey shore—territory of my childhood summers—was owned. Anyone could swim freely in the Atlantic Ocean and walk on "wet sand," the portion of the beaches that lay between high and low water marks; this belonged to the state and, therefore, to we, the people. But you had to purchase the privilege to walk along the beach or plant your shade-giving umbrella into the upper shore. During the high season between Memorial Day and Labor Day, New Jersey's coastal townships hired roving tellers to circulate with metal boxes of change, selling badges. A black badge meant you had purchased a week's worth of temporary claim. Red signified that you were a daily visitor. If you owned a house in the township, you were granted a certain number of badges as a property right. A beach house was one of the things my mother—and therefore her children—desired, but could not afford to buy.

Usually Mom paid for five badges, one for each of us, at a dollar or two a piece. We would poke the wavy copper pins on the back of the numbered plastic badges through our bathing suits, and then we were free to run to the water.

But sometimes my mother would one-up the badge lady. On those days, we'd wake extra early and arrive at the shore before lifeguards began their vigils from tall wooden chairs.

"It isn't fair to make us pay to walk on the beach," Mom would explain, circling us into a small family huddle. "So we'll just gyp them right back."

When the cashiers arrived and began to wend among the throngs, my mother would buy only three badges instead of the five that were required of our group.

"Sue, you and Bobbie slip down to the edge of the water until the lady passes by," Mom directed, as she helped the younger children fasten the pins to their suits. We knew that if a teller came our way, or a lifeguard seemed to be checking us out for the requisite tags, we were to either dive into the glacial waves, or blend into the crowds below the high tide line, the boundary above which all must pay for the privilege of access. If we needed to go up to the bathroom, or get something out of the car, one of the younger ones would lend us a badge. Paying to be on the wide open beach just didn't seem fair, and not following the rules was stressful. Even as a child I understood that limiting parking and charging for access sorted out who could or would come to the beach.

HUMANS DID NOT INVENT the concept of the beach badge. At the edge of marshy wetlands, the red-winged blackbird asserts its ownership of a nesting territory, and of one or more females, by flashing his crimson epaulet or "badge." Long ago I fell in love with a man after he told me what he did on his off hours, which was this: he would paddle the circumference of small wild ponds, all alone, locating the nests of red-winged blackbirds. In his aluminum canoe, he would observe the birds as they laid their eggs, hatched chicks, and fed and protected them until they fledged. My boyfriend insisted that the males sang out the names of their lovers. "O-da-leeeee-ska!" is how he described their territorial call. Red-winged blackbirds are polygamists, and so to avoid complications, they called all their female mates by this same ringing name. To me, it was the display of scarlet shoulder badges set against lustrous ebony feathers that assured a bird his place in the reeds.

On the fall and winter beaches along our coast, I see red-wings by the dozens, harvesting grains of sea oat. I do not look for them in the sand dunes come spring. Flaunting their fine shoulders, they will be off claiming temporary freshwater real estate for the purpose and duration of nesting.

IN 1962 my parents had finally saved enough money to purchase a strip of dune and swale on Hatteras Island in North Carolina. They subdivided the untouched property into side-by-side strips, like bacon in a frying pan, and built three rental cottages to pay off the mortgage on the land.

My father was an engineer by trade, a blacksmith and a surveyor by avocation. Certifications from the states of North Carolina, New Jersey, and Michigan allowed him to map and measure plots of land wherever we moved, a lucky thing, for the property he bought with my mother on Hatteras Island was plagued by an enormous problem: there was no access to blacktop road (probably the reason it was affordable to them). Dad eventually negotiated an easement from native Hatterasmen who owned the property between us and Highway 12, surveying and resurveying the boundaries himself with a level and transit mounted on a tripod. My brother and youngest sister took turns holding a broomstick on a chair to give my father his point of reference.

"Surveying exchanges one perspective for another," wrote Mary Clearman Blew in her memoir *All but the Waltz*, "It exchanges the physical for the abstract. As land is measured, it shrinks into its dollar equivalent . . . land loses its primacy; it becomes a resource."

LESS THAN two miles from our home in Tallahassee stands a rock and concrete structure called the principal meridian marker. Among the government buildings and the rush of downtown traffic, the heavy stone is all but hidden from view. I doubt many people have seen it. But if you own a house or a stretch of acreage in Florida, the legitimacy of your deed is entirely dependent on the integrity of this point. The original marker placed here in 1824 is known as the "Point of Beginning," and from it the state of Florida was surveyed or marked out into consecutively smaller rectangles, called sections, townships, ranges, blocks, and lots. This principal meridian, from which Tallahassee's Meridian Street takes its name, is the central north–south line used to control the integrity of the powerful, invisible system of property ownership.

When I stand at this marker, I see no natural boundaries or lines extending on the land. The meridian is an imaginary line on the Earth's surface that runs from the North Pole to the South Pole, connecting all locations in between with a given longitude. How baffling this concept of land ownership is, when nothing on the ground sets it apart as obviously distinct and to be owned in just this quantity and configuration.

Only humans have come to consider it their inherent right to buy, sell and own property either as an individual or as a member of society, or both. When land lost its primacy and came under the sway of Western legal systems, the innate rights of a territory and its inhabitants without the means to participate—a beach, a forest, a great blue heron, a fishery—fell away.

I ONCE torpedoed a Valentine's dinner by insisting on the inborn rights of a river. On that long-ago night, I sat with my date, an environmental lawyer, in a local restaurant named Chez Pierre. Candles were lit on every table, and I could smell warm bread baking.

"So I'm finishing the case for Joe Jackson regarding his Kissimmee River property," my boyfriend said, swirling a ruby-red pinot noir in his glass. I had met Jackson, a wealthy, lovely man, and liked him. I knew he wanted to develop his thousands of acres of South Florida landscape, once a rich wetland adjoining the now-channelized river, but I had fervently hoped he would not.

"Why does he have to build houses on that much land in the first place, especially in the Kissimmee's old floodplain?" I challenged.

"It's his legal right," my date replied, spreading butter on a baguette, averting his eyes from mine. "He's got a lot of money invested there. That land is now high and dry, and, if we win this case, he basically gets to do what he likes. He's a sensitive guy, he'll do a good job."

My belly tightened. "But does he truly have that right?" The candle between us guttered. Our debate intensified, turned personal. We began to speak to each other in different languages.

My date pulled back in his chair, drummed his fingers on the white-clothed tabletop. "It's simply a matter of the law, Sue," he said. "There's no other way to think about it."

"I feel sure there is a much bigger picture," I insisted, swirling a string of Gruyere cheese from the French onion soup around my spoon. Now I felt just purely mad, cornered as a bobcat by a bulldozer. My voice rose. I verged on a rant.

"What about the wood storks?" I countered, aware that I was hissing. "The herons and the egrets which have already lost most of their habitat? What about the alligators and the turtles and the Florida panthers? Don't they have rights, too?"

"Not like human landowners do," said my date. His eyes had gone distant, even cold. "Please lower your voice. Let's just drop it for now, okay?"

A waiter delivered creamy chicken crepes, but my appetite had disappeared. My companion, with advanced law degrees, was speaking entirely true to the judicial system that had trained him. But I began to realize that our legal system is a human construct, designed by humans, only for humans, certain humans, wealthy humans. I felt myself level with the river and its creatures and wasn't willing to accept that the property rights we have granted ourselves are absolute.

FOR PEOPLE, the law regarding ownership of the beach is fairly clear. Below the mean (average) high-tide line is public land, held in trust for all. If you are not a beachfront landowner, you must find access from the road to that public segment of the beach. If you do own land, you have another issue: your property line is, or will be, constantly changing. You bear the risk of losing land to erosion, or the benefit of the natural buildup of sand.

Sea turtles, shorebirds, ghost crabs, and thousands of others do not and cannot arrange their lives according to the parts of the coastline as defined by human law: wet sand or tidelands; the dry sand beach from mean high water to the vegetation line; the uplands between the dunes and the nearest road; and of course, the sea and the sea floor beyond the low-tide line. The animals orient along the edge of the sea, and have evolved over the eons in complete compliance with the movement of the coast. Their bodies are attuned to one whole and dynamic system, what some scientists call a "geologically unified wedge of sand moving up [or down] the coastal plain." Their intrinsic and genuine rights have not yet been recognized by American courts of law, not even the right to life itself. Our legal and economic systems treat the natural world as property that can be exploited and degraded, rather than as an ecological partner with its own rights to exist and thrive.

I once watched a woman collecting live sand dollars from a shallow bar off St. Mark's. She waded near me, knee-deep, fumbling for the flat rounded animals with her toes, and then pulling them to the surface of the water.

"What are you going to do with all those sand dollars?" I asked. For fear of crunching down on their shells, I had been stepping cautiously through the water column.

"I'm collecting them for party favors for my niece's wedding," the woman replied. She wiggled another palm-sized dollar free from the soft sand, and added it to the blue plastic bucket she carried.

"You know they are alive, don't you?" I asked. Her bucket brimmed with at least a hundred sand dollars. Their fine brown movable spines, which formed a feltlike coating over their shells, waved impotently in the cool air.

The woman drew back, no doubt sensing the judgment I couldn't keep out of my voice.

"Yes, I do," she said. "So I'll have to soak them in bleach and let them dry before I can paint them for table decorations."

To this day, I cannot think what more I could have said to that woman, or done.

You know they are alive, don't you?

THE DEEP PATHOLOGY of our time, wrote cultural historian Thomas Berry, is to consider our rights and our story as human beings to be different from those of the rest of creation. One of the many consequences of such thinking is that it leads us to believe that our future is unrelated to the fate of the rivers, the shorebirds, or the sand dollars.

CHAPTER 9

Claiming a Space on the Sand *Willets*

I HAVE SPENT many, many hours watching the doings of birds at the edge of the sea. Sometimes, they have been just a temporary resting place for my eyes while my brain spins its infinite scenarios, but as time passes, I observe the birds with increasing mindfulness. In my twenties, I wanted only to tell them apart, and learn their human-given names. Then I tried to keep count of what I saw. Now I am most interested in how they behave and respond to one another, and in what bits I can piece together of their lives, including the spaces they require, including the flexible, essential, and mostly invisible lines the animals draw in order to survive.

The more I learn, the more intensely I love them, and the more concern I have for their fates. How lonely I would be without them.

The willet was one of the first shorebirds I learned to identify as a young naturalist. Willets—Quaker gray with simple straight bills—were the standard against which beginning birdwatchers sorted out the ranks of other shorebirds (is the bird I am puzzling over smaller than, or larger than, a willet?). A willet can claim little physical distinction until startled into the air. But in flight, you really can't miss it. They call "Pilly-will-willet!" a three-part shriek, and their wings unfold and flash like wide white banners, or flags. Their original generic name, from the Greek, was *Catoptrophorus*. It means "carrying a mirror," referring to those brilliant wing patches. So common, so everywhere, I thought, sweeping my binoculars past the magnificent willets in search of rarer curlews or sandpipers.

But in these times of climate change and widespread extinctions, what was once common, I no longer take for granted. More and more, I stop to watch willets as they needle the surf's bubbly petticoat or wade belly-deep in pursuit of tiny worms, crabs, fish, or mollusks. Usually their prey is too small for me to see, but I have observed them snag migrating monarch butterflies just taking off over the breaking waves, short-stopping their journey to Mexico. Once Jeff and I watched a willet stalk an enormous ghost crab stranded too far from its burrow. The crab locked its stalked blackberry eyes on the bird, side-stepping every rush and foray. We could tell the battle had raged for a time, because the willet had stamped a perfect circle in the sand, with the crab at the terrible mandala's center. The bird rushed at the crab; the crab chased the bird back to the line of scrimmage. Had the crab lost its focus for even a moment, the willet's sharp forceps would have speared its carapace. The bird—which we believed would prevail by virtue of size—finally became restless and agitated, and hiked down to the tide line. We watched the crab race to a hole and vanish. I imagined the fast pump of its heart against the sand.

I have learned to look for willet castings, compacted, tubular objects shaped like the throat of the bird, which are composed of what the bird has been unable to digest. Castings are a bit stinky, and they crumble between your fingers if you handle them roughly. But they offer fascinating clues to the birds' diet, including bits of colorful coquina shell and tiny sequins of perfectly round and glittery fish scales.

I NEEDED the whole palette of the beach, empty of humans, to notice how willets, two by two, sketch winter territories in the sand. The birds I watched at Alligator Point one September day had already raised what chicks they were able earlier in the spring and summer. Often, overgrown seabird chicks, such as oystercatchers and the larger terns, will accompany and beg from one or both of their parents long after fledging. But I had never noticed this behavior among willets. Why was this pair still coupled? My curiosity and focus heightened, and soon the birds' movements distilled into discernible pattern.

The two willets stepped side by side, over the bump where high tide had dropped a load of sea grass, up onto the dry beach where ghost crabs dug their burrows and where, on weekends, human beachgoers spread their blankets. The pair was so closely synchronized, it was as if a single bird moved with its mirror image. Step, step, step. They held their heads high, necks taut, bills angled just below the horizontal. Inland they stalked, about twenty or thirty feet. The birds pivoted a half circle, touched their bills to the sand, and looped back down to the water, just as they came. Mimes might have honed the precision of their craft by watching these willets. Back and forth they strutted, drawing parallel, invisible lines in the sand, perpendicular to the sea. The empty space between them was dense and palpable, charged with territorial claim.

In and out of the willets' ritualized promenade, other kinds of shorebirds moved freely—black-bellied and semipalmated plovers, sanderlings, and ruddy turnstones, even a snowy egret. With their differentiated kinds of bills and prey preferences, they apparently were not perceived as rivals by the two willets.

Suddenly, the pair erupted into a silent aerial, twisting dogfight. Sand and feathers flew. In less than half a minute, one willet gave ground to the stronger proprietor and hunkered against the sand. Now that a hierarchy was established, both birds abandoned their struggle and returned to picking through the wrack line, no longer in any apparent competition or relationship at all. I was astonished that a bird I had once dismissed as uninteresting possessed such a fierce repertoire of ritual. From my vantage at the edge of the dunes, I scanned through my binoculars with chastened curiosity. Now that I knew what to look for, I could see pairs of willets promenading and arguing the length of Alligator Point, as far as I could see. Later, I read more about their behavior, and learned that most shorebird species exhibit varying "spacing behaviors" depending on location, time of day, and density of food resources. These rituals are ways of working out wintering territory, allowing each bird to establish and defend a limited amount of food.

Onto the stage entered a human couple, the first people I had seen that hot September morning. They powered down the beach at a fast walk, with identical water bottles slung against the small of their backs. The man wore a red ball cap backward on his head. Dark sunglasses and a broad-brimmed hat shadowed the woman's expression. The man gestured violently as he talked, his elbows chopping the air. Wind carried their voices away from me, so I couldn't hear the content of their conversation. Was this a political battle or a more personal discussion? Whichever, the couple continued down the beach, pushing through the just as intensely felt social relationships of the willets. The man and woman never noticed or acknowledged the birds. The shorebirds—not just willets, but all of them—gave way and scattered. The intricate partitioning of the beach's resources did not register with the exercising, exercised humans.

Before that day, I might not have comprehended the birds' subtle patterns, either. Why did it take me so long to see?

CHAPTER 10

What the Eagle Calls Home

"KI, KI, KI, KI," called the eagle, stuttering like a bagpipe, high and shrill. The bird stood far above my head, in a pine. A northeast breeze swayed the eagle's tree so that its needles and branchlets glittered and bobbed. Far out over the Gulf, the sun stabbed through cloud cover, lighting pools of silver. Rains would arrive later in the day, followed by cooler temperatures. The wind foretelling the front sleeked the white feathers of the eagle's head and rattled space between the snowy feathers of its tail. Unlike the migratory hawks, which seem to grow out of dead trees disguised as gnarled branchlets, eagles are all field mark, easy to spot.

What did this eagle claim as its home ground, its territory? I knew the tree above me was only one outpost in a much larger life.

The bird leaned into the prescient wind, and the feathers of its breast and forewings pressed flat against its body, as if it were dressed in articulated armor. When it shifted its stance, the breeze reparted the eagle's plumage and exposed a fresh chink in its feathers. Through my binoculars, I noticed that the long middle toe on one yoke-yellow foot ended abruptly, lacking its fearsome, curved talon. I wondered into what body that tool, that weapon— so much more than a toenail—twisted away from the eagle's foot?

The songbirds knew. They had slipped into the surrounding trees, a circle of witnesses: ring-necked doves, boat-tailed grackles, red-winged blackbirds, blue jays, and a mockingbird. Every time the eagle changed position, the smaller birds tracked him with their own bodies, alerting their community. "Thief! Thief!" shrieked the blue jay.

I shifted my binoculars to look over at the island. The pass was very quiet. Only the voices of eagles shattered the clear air. Two adults stood on the sand and contested a fish in front of the government sign that read "Point Closed to Entry." One bird stretched its head and neck up and out and screamed, and then it ripped into the fish's body with its massive bill. The second bird backed off in an awkward, rocking gait to the water's edge, waiting for what might be left. On the wildlife refuge, birds ruled the territory and sorted out their necessary boundaries between and among species, mostly without human interference. Toward the point of the island, a third eagle tilted face forward, drinking from a small rainwater pond. I continued my visual survey, amazed to count four more eagles sparring in a slow dance around an enormous dead gar at the tip of the point. Their bodies cast long, thick shadows down the beach.

Within a large, roughly circular home range (perhaps 0.5–2 square miles), a pair of adult bald eagles aggressively defended a much smaller nesting territory that would ensure enough food for their chicks. Several of these birds occupied the island's ten eagle nesting territories. Others were most likely younger individuals nomadically wandering through. Bald eagles are highly social outside of the nesting season, but extremely territorial when raising their young. I noticed both behaviors in the fall months on our coast.

The presence of so many predators explained why the hundreds of shorebirds and seabirds on the point had whirled away. Just one young dark juvenile eagle, circling vaguely, panicked a whole flock of pelicans and sent them wading into the water. They paddled in place, sketching the dimensions of the long triangular point in the surrounding waters with their bodies.

On a late afternoon in April, we dispatched down the lagoon to fish in the mouth of Big Bayou. After Jeff cut the motor, a repetitive bleating caught my ear. I thought it might be a great crested flycatcher just back from the tropics to breed. But through my binoculars I located a young bald eagle teetering on a gargantuan nest at the top of a living pine. In the fall we had seen an adult carrying a branch to add to that nest, so that she might lay her eggs around Christmas time.

Now her progeny faced into the wind, exercising its enormous untried wings. I spotted the shine of a parent's head in an adjacent tree. There was some calling back and forth: the loud rasping shriek of the young one, then the clear piping of the adult, but mostly the young voice, pleading for food.

I have observed that the nature of the eagle is to bully for its food, or scavenge, second best. It fishes and hunts its own prey as a last resort. I have watched our national bird steal from great blue herons, ring-billed gulls, black and turkey vultures, ospreys and other eagles, and I often see them working over dead carrion they find on the beach. One afternoon, Jeff and I stopped to admire a Forster's tern rise from the blue waves with a very small fish in its bill. As seabirds do, the airborne tern flipped the fish so it could slide the morsel head down and fins folded in one silky swallow. Up ahead, I saw what the tern did not—an adult bald eagle watching from a dead pine, midbeach. Like a powerful storm, the eagle lashed huge and dark at the tern, forcing the smaller bird to wrench off its flight path and relinquish its catch. The eagle snagged the tiny, nearly ungraspable fish in its yellow hunch of a bill, and carried it to a nearby tree. Through my binoculars, I watched it gulp the dainty fishlet, a shining nothing in the eagle's daily protein requirement. "That's pathetic," I said to Jeff. "Stealing baitfish from a tern!" What would have filled the stomach of the smaller bird for a time was only a pirated taste for the eagle.

Sometimes an eagle will do its own fishing. A friend watched an eagle dip down and retrieve a redfish so heavy, the bird couldn't lift it up and fly it to land. But it wouldn't let go. The bird swam its catch to shore, rowing as if its wings were oars. "That was one pooped eagle when it finally got to the beach," reported our friend. "It had to rest a while before it could haul the fish ashore!"

When an animal dies on the beach, eagles and vultures soon gain intelligence of the bounty. Once we came upon a young raccoon sprawled on the trail. Under its nose, a bit of dried blood stained the sand, although we could not tell what had caused the animal to die. Red wolf tracks encircled the body. Three days later we startled four eagles off that same carcass. No more sign of wolves. Eagles will eat meat at nearly any stage of decomposition. Wolves have a higher standard of freshness.

But eagles are not invincible: all of this territory was empty of its top raptor for most of the twentieth century. Eagles fell to the guns of sport hunters (along with many other birds), and to strychnine and DDT. Only three successful nests were found in Florida in 1958 compared to about a hundred nests just a decade earlier. The birds began to rebound after legal protections slowed their shooting in the 1940s and after the enactment of a ban on the use of DDT. Bald eagles are no longer listed as endangered.

My colleague Barbara Stedman, a longtime observer of area birds, told me that St. Vincent was the very first place eagles nested in Florida as they began to recover from the DDT population crash in the 1960s. Now, between Port St. Joe and Apalachicola, there are at least twenty-five eagle nests, including ten on St. Vincent Island. Bald eagles have reclaimed their entire historic range in Florida. I am one of the fortunate observers of this miracle.

"KI, KI, KI, KI," the eagle called as she landed, soaking wet, in the tree over my head. I didn't know whether she had been fishing or bathing, but I watched her tend her feathers. As she wrung each stocky chocolate quill through her massive gold beak, droplets of water spackled the branch below her perch. She relaxed her wings so that they hung like a cape; her joints and tail appeared to nearly detach, allowing her to swivel and attend all the way to the base of her plumes. One by one, she squeezed each white tail feather, kneading and spreading fatty oil from a gland in the base of her tail. When her grooming was complete, she roused and ruffled in a whole body shake. Her feathers stood on end, knocking together like thin bones, the wind fingering them dry.

"Ki, ki, ki, ki, ki, ki, ki!" piped the eagle in the pine. One tribe of Native Americans—the Crow—interpreted the eagle's call as follows:

We want what is real.

We want what is real.

Don't deceive us

For at least three thousand years, native people in the South incised the images of eagles and other raptors on wood, stone, shell, and pottery—more so than any other order or family of birds. Fans made of eagle feathers were used in ceremony, as were their claws and talons. In narrative, religion, and politics, the authority of the eagle loomed large.

"Kleek keek keek!" I replied, mimicking best I could. "Kleek keek keek!" What I wanted to communicate was that I craved what was real, too. If the eagles' expansive territories remained intact, then there would be enough wildness for the rest of us as well.

The bird looked down at me on the porch below the pine. Its glance was a glare. Into the air it jumped, stroking over the body of the pass. The press of St. Vincent's warm breath lifted the bird still higher. I watched the eagle climb the clouds and join two others of its kind. The trio traced the vast sweep of the sky, revolving as if strung on a mobile suspended from the day-bleached moon. The point and the pass and the Gulf were all one seamless fabric, one home range, from their vantage. So widely they lived on these islands, in territories I could not see, but we could share.

CHAPTER 11

The Rights of Birds

ALONG OUR COAST, least terns begin to breed in March, in a state of great urgency. To tempt their mates, male terns target bright tiny fish that row through the prism of the tide. But the fishlets are devoted to their own silver seasons, and they fling their bodies through the pass, granting the birds no slack. The tern will not catch his dinner through chance encounter; he must employ an equal desire, matching his beak and his aim to the profound fleeing of the fish.

Think of being a baitfish, with pelicans and terns crashing at you from above, from air and sky you don't even know exist. It seems like fear would define your very life. The universe heaves fierce flying creatures through the water, and toothy sharks and bluefish pick you off from below. What becomes of the baitfish's temperament—the singular spirit that enlivens it—as its body is transmuted into tern?

One evening I floated in my kayak near a place where least terns nest on the shore. I chose a distance that would not disturb a pair of birds courting on the shining sand. The female shirred her wings, fluttering soft like a dove, the very image of receptivity. The male stood before her. His bill pinched a living fish the size of a soupspoon. As he moved his head side to side to tempt his mate, the last angling of the sun struck the body of the fish. My breath caught: it appeared that the tern offered elemental silver to his mate. She accepted his nourishment, both actual and ritual. Fish dies into bird, bird fertilizes an egg, and life proceeds through the intricate lovemaking of terns, and the sacrifice of small fish. The terns bind one to another, vowing to protect and feed a pair of chicks until they can arrow the waters from the bow of the air, and confidently obtain food for themselves.

And as I watched them, I saw with fresh eyes how delicately they defined and claimed the space they need to survive. This they do with only the instruments of voice, ritual, and body. The birds don't need us in any way to contribute to their living year, except to staunch their extinguishing. We must protect some places sacrosanct for them.

ONE SEPTEMBER MORNING, I watched a small group of shorebirds foraging at the edge of the water: three willets, a black-bellied plover, a sanderling, and two ruddy turnstones. Between me and the shorebirds, lines of multiple tire tracks pressed the sand flat. The strand was a road offered to anyone willing to purchase an inexpensive permit from Gulf County.

All shorebirds genuflect to the water when they seek their prey. They are built to bow to the beach. But the black-bellied plover, with its ebony armpits and a very short, stout bill, spent far less time foraging than the others. Here is how it moved: step, step, step, pause, watchfully look about. Step, step, step, pause, survey the scene for danger. One of the willets dominated the others, threatening its two conspecifics with a wide-open bill. This was a dance all of the birds understood, and they adjusted their complex proximity smoothly, without overly disturbing any of the birds from their feeding. The other species maintained a close, elastic distance, prodding in their own ways at the lapping edge of the pass. About four dozen black skimmers folded into the little mixed flock, landing, taking off, circling, skittish, worried. They fit themselves into the spaces between the willets and all the others. Each skimmer faced the water; as they stood on the beach, the backs of their heads appeared to have short razor-sharp haircuts, black caps over exposed white necks—almost punk. Funny! With the sudden gabble, a light nasal honking, the skimmers took to the air one last time, leaving empty spaces behind. The willets were left surrounded by the absence of skimmers.

Shorebirds need the beach for sleeping, feather care, eating, and nesting. The restive and rare birds—oystercatchers, red knots, curlews, and certain plovers—are the first to be displaced. Willets and sanderlings will sometimes skip ahead and then double back to the same feeding spot after danger passes, but the shyest species will not. Human disturbance renders the beach almost unusable to its original inhabitants.

Minutes before people appeared in my view, walking on the beach, I knew they were coming. The birds in my small flock began to startle and alert, shuffling their feet, ceasing to feed. More shorebirds crowded into view. Sanderlings swirled in groups of six or eight, closer than they wanted to be to one another. Oystercatchers piped single syllable alert calls, and came quick-stepping down the beach until they couldn't stand the tension any longer. Then they jumped into their wings and circled out over the water to search out a quieter place. What is it that the birds fear so much in our slow upright straight-path walking?

Now I could see the source of the birds' discomfiture. A couple holding hands approached from the boat ramp, and a woman with a small poodle on a leash moved our way from the west. The black-bellied plover, always the least tolerant to a threat, began to whistle and bob its head. The birds herded more tightly together, but finally they all gave way, objects without standing. In panicked flight, these wild birds were no longer in relationship, or feeding and meeting their subsistence needs. The beach goers did not notice. I suspect they didn't realize that disrupting birds from feeding, resting or ritual is of consequence. The edge of the beach is for people to walk along as and when they please. The birds must give way to our oblivion.

AROUND THE AUTUMN EQUINOX, I have often counted eight or nine hundred brown pelicans at the point of Indian Pass. They begin to muster at the edge of the water just after dawn. Like flakes of fire ash, dozens of black skimmers join the masses at the point. Synchronized by strong group mind, black skimmers seem all of a piece, torn from the same ebony template. Intermingled among the pelicans and skimmers, scarves of terns, gulls, and small shorebirds wrap themselves around the island's neck. Through my scope, I watch the care and attention the birds allot to each feather: flattening, arranging, pulling, and smoothing, spreading fatty oil from a gland in their tails to fashion a water-proof cloak.

But if I see the birds swirling into the air, describing currents in space with their bodies, I know that something has scared them from the refuge. How many and what kinds of birds flush depends on the level of threat they perceive and can tolerate.

Sometimes I noticed only the terns (five kinds! Caspian, royal, Forster's, sandwich, and least!) and gulls and skimmers—just the midsized white birds—flushed from the avian congregations on the point. They lifted away into the air, leaving behind what resembled a pelican statue garden, circling fast, uttering mingled, interspecies alarm calls. I looked for the body type and movement that seemed not to belong, appeared different in that beautiful, shaken snow globe. Often it was a dark and fierce peregrine falcon, face marked like a bandit, migrated in from somewhere west and north, hungry, fast, hunting. The terns circled tightly together, and the falcon chased the outliers.

Other times every one of the many hundreds of skimmers and terns and pelicans are shaken from the sand like long lengths of billowing fabric. The heavier-bodied pelicans take a short lap and then resettle, some on the water and some on the beach. What caused such upset? Ah, I see it: a single eagle, circling the point.

Even on refuge lands, the birds have no absolute protection, despite the most important law passed on behalf of wildlife in the last half-century: the Endangered Species Act. The act only works well when someone is caught shooting or otherwise killing an endangered bird. How do we know it is not enough? Bird populations are plummeting nationwide and planetwide. When I watch the complete displacement of one thousand pelicans, and hundreds of skimmers and other shore and seabirds from the point, I can tell humans have transgressed into their refuge. It might be a trio of bicyclists carried to the island by a boat, pushing along the sand path to the beach. Other times people—sometimes traveling by kayak from one of the rental houses, or the campground, or dropped off by the concessionaire—walk around the point, despite the protective signage. My level of upset and irritation cannot match that of the birds, for they own nowhere, can count on no place to rest undisturbed, even in the refuge established specifically for their protection. And sometimes I have watched people run at the rare congregations of birds, just to see them fly, or to take pictures, reducing the living beings to mere spectacle.

IT COMES DOWN TO THIS: We have no cultural commitment to safeguarding the places the shorebirds live—their habitat—except during nesting season, when wildlife managers string plastic yellow rope between upright lengths of PVC pipe, symbolic or virtual fencing on the wide-open beach where the birds are laying eggs. Here's a human analogy. It's as if only certain races of humans, and only the places where they give birth at that, were protected. I don't believe there will ever be more security for wild things until we can see how their needs and their lives parallel our own.

LAST FALL, my friend Crystal and I sat together on the high porch of a rental house overlooking Indian Pass. The morning was absolutely clear. It seemed as though we could reach out and touch the island across the water. I hooked my feet over the wooden rail, binoculars and bird book at the ready. We still wore our nightclothes, and billed caps to shade our eyes from the sun.

"Hey, those are red knots!" I said to Crystal, pointing to a group of birds on our beach. "Seventeen of them!" That highly endangered long-distance migrant was not one of the birds my friend could yet identify.

"How do you tell them?" she asked, pressing her binoculars against her eyes.

"Red knots are larger than sanderlings, and smaller than the willets, with a very sturdy build. They feed in the same wet sand, and they are always voraciously hungry. When I see a group of them, they remind me of a row of carbon copies. They are the opposite of black-bellied plovers, which like to feed alone." As I talked, Crystal studied the birds with her optics.

"See how they crowd and bunch along the beach, shoulder to shoulder? To me, they have sort of a harassed vibe." I said. "We only see them briefly as they migrate through. They are in a hurry to get on to their next stopover place."

Suddenly, a medium-sized black dog hurtled across the beach in front of us, panicking every one of the red knots into flight. As dogs generally are, this one seemed pleased with himself and waded into the water up to his chest, longing to chase the birds still further. He lapped saltwater, breathed hard, wagged his tail. Trailing far behind was his owner, a tall slim woman who seemed deep in thought or maybe talking on her cell phone.

"Crystal, please, please go down and ask that woman to put her dog on a leash," I begged my friend. "I am so upset, I'm sure I wouldn't handle it well."

"But I am wearing SpongeBob SquarePants pajamas," said Crystal. "And what would I say to her? I'm no expert. How will I get her to take me seriously?"

"Please? I know you'll think of a friendlier way to explain the problem than I can right now."

Bless her heart, Crystal took the long steps down to the beach at a fast clip, and intercepted the lean woman as she passed in front of our house.

"Hi, I know this is awkward, and I hope you take it the right way," Crystal said to the stranger. "I just need you to know that those little birds your dog is chasing are hungry. They've come all the way from the Arctic Circle, and they still have to fly all the way to Patagonia. This beach is the only place they can get their food. We have a choice about where we walk, and what our dogs do, but these birds don't."

From what I could see, the woman looked startled, but not unfriendly.

After a moment's thought, she replied, "The thing is, I chose this beach specifically because the advertising for my rental house said my dog could run free." The black mutt circled the two of them as they talked, wriggling in excitement, grinning his goofy joy.

"I understand," said Crystal. "It's just that the birds really need a chance to feed here. Thanks for hearing me out."

"How did she take it? Do you think she got it?" I asked my friend when she had rejoined me on the porch.

"It was a little weird, but I just tried to put myself in her place," Crystal replied. "I showed her the pelicans hanging out on the wildlife refuge over there on the point, and I could see she was kind of thinking, well, that place is for the birds, so can't this beach just be for people and their dogs? I didn't get into how this side of the pass has more of what the birds need to eat.

"She did say she'd walk her dog down the other way from our cabin during her visit," Crystal added. "I'm pretty sure she is respectful of our needs as bird lovers, but I really don't think she got the urgency of it from the red knot's perspective."

SEVERAL DAYS LATER, I watched two women, a small child, and two Pomeranian dogs come strolling down the same beach. The boy had brown curls and a very straight back. He was dressed in a red sweatshirt, black high-top sneakers, and loose blue flannel pants, pushed up over his knees. At the water's edge, a flock of ruddy turnstones, three dozen or more, gleaned their food from the sand.

The boy trudged head down: maybe he felt listless, or more likely he just didn't want to walk a straight line. But his mother and her friend craved exercise. The friend was snapping pictures with a big camera, too.

The child came upon a long loose feather, probably shed by a pelican, and he held it out in front of him like a wand, experimenting with the feel of its resistance through the air. His mother became impatient. She wanted to get her son moving faster. She spotted the feeding shorebirds.

"Chase the birdies, Dominic!" she called to her son, thinking to leapfrog her child down the beach by having him pursue pods of timid birds.

"Run after them, Dominic! Go get 'em!" And so he did, and so they all flew, abandoning their breakfast foraging.

The child was not ill intended. His instinct was to follow his mother's instructions and to run closer to those who wore feathers and moved in such an interesting manner. Neither, I suppose, was the mother ill intended, although she taught her son what she must have learned herself: that wild birds are Other—they are Objects, not equivalent to a child or a lapdog, in terms of satisfying their hunger free from fear.

What poverty of imagination, I thought to myself, sadly. I wanted to ask the woman, "Why?" but all that came to me was: "Stop it! What is the matter with you people?" And I knew that wouldn't be helpful. So I kept watching, trying to see what I might learn.

Dominic began to harvest small shells from the sand and experimented with placing them at the edge of the water. He was curious about how things interplayed in his world. Small waves generated by the wake of a boat washed over his feet and the shells. I heard him chortle.

"All right that's enough, Dominic, you're getting soaked," called his mom. "Look, there are more birds down the beach!" The only way his mother seemed to imagine moving him through the landscape was by forcing birds to fly.

The woman's friend began to photograph a great blue heron in the slash pine at the bottom of a dune. "Look at him, with the sun shining on his feathers!" Ah, this is better, I thought.

"Dominic!" they called. "Look at that big bird! Watch how it turns its head to the side!" But the child was half the height of the heron, and the heron too far up in the tree for the boy to really see.

The boy's focus, his moment, was much closer to his small body. The opportunity for bird appreciation was lost. Instead, Dominic would remember to hurry and to mindlessly chase after whatever it is that moves on the beach.

Were we to evolve into a just world, the mother (or father) would seize that very moment when the child sights the group of wild birds and points with a feather he has retrieved from the sand. She would kneel and encircle his waist, holding him close to her body while the warm waves swashed around their feet. She would know that once an experience is embedded in story and body, it can be absorbed and passed on to the next generation. So the mother would tell him a tale that would impress upon him the sacred equivalent rights of the birds, their needs and their lives, so that he himself could move forward respectfully within the community of life.

Such a shift in consciousness will demand heroic effort. We will have to radically redefine our identities, our habits, and our priorities with respect to all of the Earth. What will successfully motivate us is neither obligation nor fear, but our love for our children and for the beauty of all the beings of the Earth. We—I—will have to learn to speak of these matters with courage and kindness on behalf of the birds.

I recently dreamed that I was driving along a dangerous downhill road, weaving in and around potholes. As I rounded a blind curve, I was shocked to come upon the live torsos of animals. They looked like foxes or meerkats. The animals were only half emerged from the asphalt. Their lower torsos were hidden under the pavement, covered over or crushed. I could see that they were trapped, but somehow still alive. Their big round mammal eyes stared at me, mute and suffering. Down the blacktop, I could see there were many more of them in my path.

I believe my dream speaks truly. We humans are in the drivers' seats, living such fast and frenetic lives that we cannot slow down to see, let alone stop, the way we literally "run over" other creatures who coinhabit this Earth. But perhaps the dream figures also represent how we ourselves are stuck in oil-and-gas-underwritten lifestyles. Many of us want to slow down and connect with what really matters most to us. But that can happen only if we renounce the ways we habitually move about in space.

What if we tried to imagine ourselves as those animals, mired in the asphalt? What if we said to ourselves, "I'm stuck here in this situation and it doesn't seem promising. But perhaps I can wriggle free. I've got some tools still to work with: arms, heart, brain, eyes, ears."

It is right and necessary to do.

To honor the needs of shorebirds I have developed a meandering way of walking on the beach. I don't stride straight down the wrack line or the line of the tide when birds are there before me. When I come upon a feeding or resting flock of birds, I loop around them toward the dunes, as far away as their comfort requires. Then I return to the edge of the water. Moving mindfully around the lives and territories of animals we share the space with can free our own minds from self-absorption.

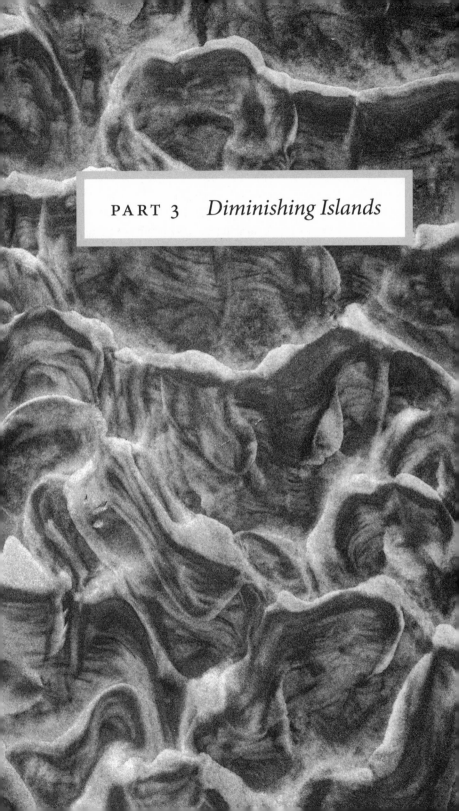

PART 3   *Diminishing Islands*

Our beloved coast is changing in response to rapid, overwhelming human forces. Sometimes we target a species for profit or sport—fish, birds, even sand dollars. Sometimes we appropriate their habitat so that we can build beachfront homes or other structures. For profit or convenience, we mine fresh water from the rivers or the aquifers, oil from deep under the Gulf, and even erase the darkness from the night. All of our taking and using has resulted in the diminishment of the coast's biodiversity and is severely disrupting our once stable climate.

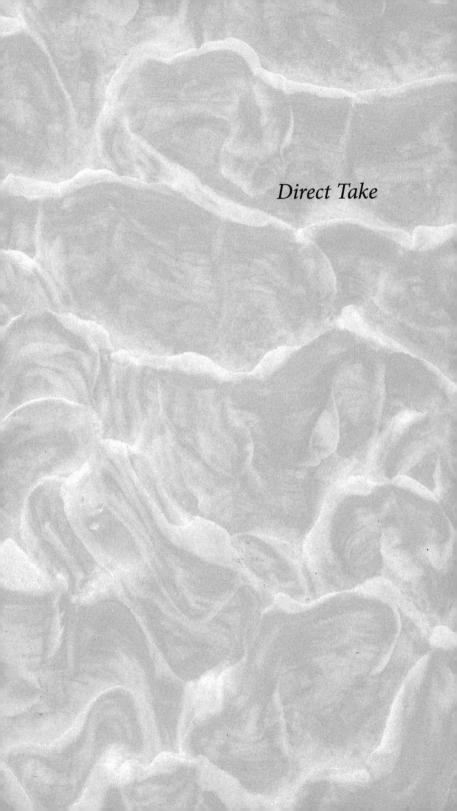

Direct Take

CHAPTER 12

The Ways We Fish

ON A MORNING early in December, I stalked the shore of Indian Pass with a shrimp net and practiced the circle of my toss, which meant that my eyes were on the water at the moment it came twitching alive. There weren't many fish at first, only a few fins and tails turning and sparkling at the surface. But within minutes, the fish—mullet, I could tell—coalesced into broad riffling rafts in numbers I'd never witnessed before, here at the pass, or anywhere. It seemed like something out of a dream. The circles of fish—slap, slap, slapping—wheeled slowly past me toward the Gulf. Their course took them out with the tide.

"The mullet is an obliging kind of fish," a Wakulla County fisherman once told me. "It's almost like they want to get caught, the way they swim from east to west when they run along the beach." The particular mullet I was watching were definitely swimming east to west, lagoon to Gulf, with their "right eyes to the hill (or shore)," as the man had explained.

"Come quick, bring the big net!" I called up to Jeff at the cabin. "Hurry, hurry, the mullet are running!"

Jeff took the steps two at a time, swinging a five-gallon white plastic bucket and the long-braille net we'd ordered from Memphis Net and Twine.

A green Chevy Blazer came rattling down from the boat ramp. The enormous man at the wheel braked hard, grabbed his net from the passenger seat, and shouldered beside us at the edge of the water.

"Name's Jimbo," he said, as he let fly over the fish. His net was as long as his body was tall, weighted at bottom with a chain-link strand. Jimbo's face was shadowed by a salt-stained black cap and polarized sunglasses. "Don't even come out here without polarized if you're going to fish," he said. The man brimmed with commentary and advice, as hand over hand, he reeled his catch in to shore.

"Here, feel of it," Jimbo said to Jeff. "I can't even hold it off the ground with one hand. It weighs about twenty pounds!" And considerably more after it was threaded with a half dozen mullet, which, after the second throw, it was.

"I'm used to the jump of a mullet or two at a time, but I've never seen anything like this," I said to Jimbo.

"Know how I knew this was going to happen?" he replied. It was hard to understand his words. He held the edge of his net in between his teeth as he prepared to throw it out over the press of fish. "There were two acres of mullet in the lagoon back behind my house yesterday. I couldn't get to them with my boat. It was just too shallow."

Jeff hauled in his own net and found it folded around the silvery struggle of eight or nine keepers. On just one cast. My light shrimp net was of no use with these heavy fish, so I dropped it on the beach and helped Jeff untangle what he'd caught.

Jeff was snaring more fish than he ever had before in his life, but still Jimbo had ideas about refining his technique.

"Don't wade out when you throw, Jeff," Jimbo called. My husband was gathering his net for another throw, standing shin-deep in the water. "The fish will feel the vibrations and move away."

Presently, a dozen or more local dolphins joined the scene. It was clear that neither the mullet nor the dolphins cared anything about us, our whirling nets, or how far out we waded. The dolphins maneuvered the schooling fish into a tight panicked circle the size of half a tennis court, beyond the reach of our casting.

"Sometimes those boys will rush the mullet right up to shore into your net," Jimbo said hopefully.

For just a moment, the big animals herded the fish almost to our beach with powerful thrusting arcs of their bodies. The men prepared to throw, but just then the dolphins directed the run right back out into the pass, managing the mullet through a primitive, powerful terror, more like armed guards than Flipper. It felt like the original struggle between wild predator and prey. For the moment, the three of us on shore were irrelevant.

"Those bastards will eat five hundred pounds a day." Jimbo scowled and paced, no longer friendly toward the dolphins. They were competing too successfully with his efforts.

There was nothing else we could do, so we watched how the mullet ran, and the phenomenal frenzy of dolphins and pelicans that surrounded them.

"You only see the males jump," said Jimbo, lighting up a cigarette. "They might be taking a look around, or they might be just traveling." Jimbo might just be making this up, I thought. "The females are deeper beneath the water, spawning." Driven by the night's projected temperatures—near freezing—all those thousands of fish were headed offshore toward warmer waters, to lay their eggs.

Word of the mullet run had spread. A handful of fishing skiffs—three and four men apiece—launched at the ramp and powered into the pass, casting over the fish from their boats.

"Those guys are using short-braille nets," said Jimbo. "Charlie Amons over in Port St. Joe makes them special with chain-link instead of weights around the bottom of the net." He studied Jeff's net. "See you've got a long-braille net, Jeff. That's not nearly as good." At this point the fish were well out of reach of our net and Jimbo's too. We watched the men in boats throw their nets, one after the next, then haul them hand over hand quickly from the water. The fishermen whooped and hollered. We could hear the stout bodies of their captives thunk against the metal bottoms of the boats. They tossed back the smaller, sleeker white roe males, filling their coolers only with red roe–bearing females. I heard one man speculate that he would get thirty cents a pound for white roe, considerably more for red. He was thinking pounds of fish translated into dollars at the market later today.

I fetched my filet knife and a white plastic cutting board and prepared to clean our fish for dinner, admiring the sturdy cut of their bodies. The mullet is armored with scales as wide and substantial as its head. It looks like it was made to hammer its way through something denser than seawater, so blunt and broad is its body.

THE HARDEST PART about cleaning a fish is the time before it is dead. I don't like it; Jeff won't do it. But to eat an animal you catch, you've got to face up to its dying. I began by severing the first fish's head with strong bloody diagonal slices, hoping to shorten its suffering. This one was a female, a good third larger and heavier than the males. Her roe—the eggs of new life short-stopped by our net—lay like enormous orange sausages in her abdominal cavity. More egg than flesh, she had intended to spawn offshore tonight.

The egg of a mullet is a tiny thing, smaller than the tip of a pencil, yet filled with the purpose of becoming fish. Mother mullet bear over a half-million such ova, transparent and tinted the color of straw. In the heart of each lies one buoyant and round globule of oil. For a mullet egg to become fish, the parents and their offspring require the whole range of our coastal waters. Through the estuaries and passes, the fish make their essential journey to spawn. The deep gulf raises up the eggs and larvae. Salt creeks and marshes allow the juvenile mullet to fatten and grow.

Cold winter air dug under my collar as I squatted over my task. The weather had been changing all morning: a sprinkle, some sun, another stretch of cloud. Now we could feel the north wind settling in with purpose.

My cell phone buzzed in the pocket of my shorts. Jeff dug out the phone for me and turned on the speaker, since I was wrist deep in guts and scales and roe.

"Hi, Mom!" It was my son David, calling from his college up in Connecticut. "I wish you could see the ice covering all the trees—it looks like there are amazing ice sculptures outside every window." The same cold front that had coated New England with sleet and ice was driving these mullet through Indian Pass. I liked thinking that this one powerful weather system linked me to my grown child, even though we were a thousand miles apart.

Out in the pass, the three boats of anglers returned again and again to the ramp, unloading their coolers into their trucks. It was hard not to get swept up in the moment of utter plenty. Even the two of us, after catching twenty fish—mostly in just a couple of prodigious throws by Jeff—considered launching our own boat at the ramp and joining the others in the pass. But we'd caught as many mullet as we thought we could eat or give away to friends.

Down on the beach, Jimbo slapped the covers on a pair of enormous coolers in the back of his vehicle.

"These are 'for Mama,'" he said, with a wink. He'd told us that a person is only allowed to keep fifty fish a day, unless they had purchased a commercial license, and I was pretty sure Jimbo's Mama couldn't throw a net. So we knew he meant this was a way to get around the rules, limits designed to keep mullet populations at a healthy number.

As I washed up my cutting board at the edge of the water, I called over to a man working alone in a flat-bottom metal skiff equipped with a forty-horsepower Mercury motor.

"How often do you see a run like this?"

"Once a year," he said. "I was cat fishing on the river when I got the call. I had shot me three squirrels, but I came on over here as quick I could when I heard about the run." The angler wore a tomato red sweatshirt and brown khaki pants, looked to be in his sixties. He told us he was the volunteer fire chief from Apalachicola. He struggled alone with his skiff, the motor, his net, and the swift tide, but he seemed really happy.

"This is the most fish I've ever caught in my life," he said, before turning back to his task. "If I catch enough, I'll have a benefit fish fry for the department."

Hours later, Jeff and I sat together in our warm rented cottage on the hill, using forks and then our fingers, digging the thick and sweet backbone meat from our fish straight off a single pan we'd carried in from the grill on the deck. We'd executed Jimbo's last suggestion to us before he took off down the beach: butterfly-fillet the mullet and grill it in a foil boat with butter and lots of garlic.

Out in the dusk, I could see that the fire chief was the last man on the pass. He was still throwing that net.

AT THE COAST, there is always opportunity to contemplate the matter of "taking," whether I want to think about it or not. Too often, our human relationship with fish and shrimp is unhealthy for the individual species, the ocean community, or both.

How do we know how much we can take? How do we control ourselves in the absence of clear answers? I believe when the impulse to take becomes industrialized by corporations, the wounds to life become intolerable. A single fisherman netting more than his limit with a wink and a lie doesn't dismantle a fishery, but the inclination to cheat may, in the long run. What absolutely will destroy a race of fish is when that impulse to greed is lashed together with the huge legal and technological power of corporations. Avarice is at the root of the misappropriation of everything from oil and gas to fresh water, from fisheries to the integrity of Earth's gene pools. We must look for the signs in ourselves, both of the tendency to gluttony, and the tendency to love and to tend.

AT THE DARK END of a winter's day, Jeff and I made our way down to the boat ramp with the idea of netting some shrimp for our dinner. As we approached the concrete revetment, I noticed a single fisherman and worried that we would disturb his solitude.

And we did.

"Awwkkk!" croaked the angler—a lanky-legged great blue heron. The bird wheeled away into the dusk.

Jeff hoped to recreate a shrimping technique from his Biloxi childhood. We set up a gas Coleman lantern at the end of the ramp. Jeff had mashed up a chum of cornmeal mixed with canned dog food (which those Mississippi shrimp had never been able to resist). He scattered it into the current. The idea was that the light and the food would draw the shrimp within casting range of our net. We allowed the chum to settle, then took turns launching the net out over the black water. Quicksilvery baitfish filled the mesh, gleaming, and we also caught a needlefish and a small squid, which bit Jeff's finger as he disentangled it. These were our bycatch, all of which we were able to return to the water alive. Shrimp were the rarest of what we captured, a couple dozen decent-sized browns.

When we returned to our rented cabin, we sprayed the net clean with fresh water and then sautéed our few shrimp with a bit of olive oil, diced garlic, and green peppers we had grown in our garden back home. The kitchen filled with steam and fragrance.

We woke the next morning to the deep grind of motors out in the pass. The run of shrimp from which we had withdrawn our supper had attracted trawlers. They pocketed the mouth of the pass. Four were small enough to launch from the county ramp, and one was an enormous industrial boat. What could avoid their nets?

Consider the matter of scale. There is me with my scant net. There is the sky-blue local boat—small scale, jerry rigged, and homemade—sieving the pass's outgoing tide with its nets. There is the industrial trawler lit up all night, outshining Venus, and discarding five or more pounds of fish and other sea life for every pound of shrimp it nets. Then there are the winter resident red-breasted mergansers, built for sleek feeding on the shrimp. Who is to say, who will decide, which of us takes too much?

Our bodies, our senses can offer us insights. I am standing on the beach at the mouth of the pass, and the day is unusually still. I hear willets competing for territory. I hear phoebes up in the dunes. The cast netter's shoes crunch on the shell wash, and when his net connects with the water, there is the sound of plopping and splash. The loudest noise I hear travels the furthest distance: winches on the trawlers taking shrimp at least a mile out in the

Gulf. The creaking of the winches and the grind of the trawlers' engines don't fit in with the other sounds of the world here. It is a continuous heavy growl, one low pitch fueled by diesel, with the power to take inconsistent with any kind of reasonable harvest. The vibration of the trawlers only fades if the wind redirects the passage of that sound over the water. The trawler relentlessly appropriates. It only stops when its nets are full. According to stock assessments completed for NOAA in 2012, Gulf of Mexico pink shrimp are not overfished. But the bottom trawls these fishermen use to catch shrimp harm the floor of the Gulf, and they also capture and kill many, many other species. The trawlers discard that wondrous spread of juvenile red snapper, mackerel, crabs, flounder, spot, and hundreds of others entrapped by the nets. Most die. The trawlers feed the swarms of gulls that surround them like giant flies. They feed people—sometimes me—who buy the shrimp. And they feed their corporate owners. Money is exchanged for life. My senses tell me how different this kind of fishing is from the sustainable take of, say, the brown pelican.

I HAVE ONLY SEEN the before and the long after of shark fishing. I have watched people hire a boat to kill sharks they will not eat. I have watched them return to the dock, shovel a dead nurse shark on the boat ramp, only three and a half feet long, and pose their children in front of the murdered animal. I have seen the exaggerated fear of the children, and the hard set of the father's faces, watching. There have been no recorded shark attacks in the Big Bend since 1882, according to the University of Florida's 1882–2012 map of Florida's confirmed unprovoked shark attacks. And yet our fear of sharks is colossal.

One time, as we fished from our boat off one of the passes, the surface of the water began to dimple as if it were raining, only upward, rain falling up from below. Or, as if someone were underneath the surface of the water, snapping their fingers and creating hundreds and hundreds of tiny ripples. But it was the mouths of small fishes that riddled the water, petite baitfish called menhaden. People also call them pogies.

The weather had been dry, so the water was very, very clear. As I cast my line, I could see below our boat the whole food chain in action. Bluefish darting after pogies. Pelicans twisting from the sky, also lunging after pogies. Dolphins chasing bluefish. And then as we stayed on, sharks materialized, small ones but lots of them, to pick off whatever they could. It was a magnificent sight. And yet of all the beings pursuing and pursued, only the sharks generated a thrill of fear.

Along our coast, bull, black tip, sharpnose, nurse, and even tiger sharks are sought by sport-eager anglers when inshore waters warm and the baitfish multiply. Anglers target the sharks for the fight, and sometimes for food.

Sometimes I see groups of young men set up a serious shark-fishing endeavor, as if they went to war along Indian Pass. They work twenty-four-hour shifts, ignoring sunburn and biting insects. They keep lanterns burning all night long. They set up stout rods at intervals along the beach in PVC holders. Fishing tackle for sharks requires heavy wire leaders ten to fifteen feet long; large, sharp hooks; and heavy line, lots of line. The beach seems less safe to me when the shark fishermen are there. In parts of the country, in response to drastically diminishing shark populations, anglers are turning to catch-and-release contests. They use circle hooks, which are said to damage the mouths of sharks less than a traditional hook. Still, you are piercing an animal's mouth and dragging it through the water, tiring it out sometimes to the point of death. And this we call a sport.

I AM AMONG the many people who fish because it keeps me outside with the purpose of procuring food from its original source, not from a grocery store. In the catching, cleaning, and cooking, I restore myself within the cycles of my place. One October day I watched a man wading thigh-deep in the edge of Indian Pass, heaving his line. A heavy fanny pack cinched around his waist held everything he would need to fish. No car, no cart, no tackle box, just what he could carry on his body. The angler was one with the water and the fish, so silky was his cast, so constantly dancing and adjusting were his arms and his torso and his legs. In the time it took me to draw up close, I saw him catch and then let go two huge pink-bodied redfish. I stopped to watch as he reeled in a third, his light pole straining under the arc.

"Easy now," he said to the fish, clamping its body between his upper arm and his rib cage. With great care, he disengaged the hook from the animal's jaw.

"Redfish enter the pass on incoming tides in the fall to lay their eggs," he explained when I asked how he knew when to come to this place. "The tide pulls the eggs into the salt marshes lining the lagoon, and there they grow, or are themselves eaten."

The man lowered the quivering fish into the water, and I returned to my walking. I had no urge to join him in his sport of catch and release, but I was glad to know more of what was happening out of sight, under the pass.

CHAPTER 13

Oystercatchers

AT SUMMER'S CLOSE, American oystercatchers lead their young to our Gulf beaches, favoring the drop of the tide. Clothed in short, wide hoopskirts of ebony feathers over pale pink legs, these large shorebirds forage without comment among clutches of ruddy turnstones and sanderlings. But when one of their own kind flies by, "Wheep," they cry, a whistling call of contact. They stay only as long as the shore is free of dogs and people.

Observing the intimate lives of wild birds affords me deep pleasure, but this wary species will not tolerate me creeping as close as I'd like to be, and I try to respect their requirements. One day I walked far down the beach and then floated back to a group of oystercatchers on an old boat cushion, about twenty feet out from shore. My chin rested on the canvas. My profile was just at the height of the small waves. The sun rose like a biscuit in the oven that was September's sky. It felt so good to be immersed.

So far, I was not disturbing the oystercatchers as they brought up small clams from the tide line with their stout, vermillion bills. One bird bent over so far, it stood nearly on its head to tease out prey. I could see that they were harvesting coquinas. The pastel mollusks upended as each wave retreated and pulled the sand off their bodies. They resembled a host of a small, smooth buttocks lowering briskly into the sand. Down the beach the birds had left a trail of empty coquina shells, angled wings of tiny angels, glistening on the sand. Later I retrieved a handful and breathed in their salty fragrance through my nose. I was grateful to raft along with the oystercatchers, sensing into their lifeways without guidebook or binoculars between us.

Female oystercatchers are slightly larger than males, although they are otherwise indistinguishable from their mates. I could easily tell first year chicks from their parents. The juveniles' bills were dusky charcoal—they hadn't yet grown into their color. Maybe that's a bit of evolutionary protection. A predator might not notice a smoke-colored bill on the beach like it would the adult's flamboyant watermelon proboscis. And the inexperienced young were playful and a bit clumsy. Unlike other shorebird chicks, oystercatchers cannot feed themselves until well after fledging. These callow chicks shadowed their parents, probing into holes the older birds mined in the sand. They dug to learn the preferred depths of mollusks and worms. I smiled, watching a juvenile pick unfruitfully at sticks, bits of seaweed, and empty cockleshells at the wrack line. None of these would fill his stomach. The big baby approached a parent, nudging up under its belly like a petulant calf butting at the teats of a cow. The intimate demand of the young bird was almost mammalian, a gesture of attachment as real as the long-ago nuzzle of my own baby when he wanted to nurse. The older birds watched for danger as they shucked clams for their chicks. Any human parent would relate to their unstinting effort and to their caution. Later in the fall, oystercatchers would gather up by the dozens, standing flat-footed in the surging foam on the front of the island. The dark-billed juveniles would continue to plea for food, with distraught wide-open cries. But by then, their parents would have completed their tending.

For the moment, I was deeply happy to scull quietly and blend as best I could into the sea, even though the warm salt water was shriveling my skin. I tried to project myself as completely non-threatening, hoping that the cautious, black-cloaked family would stay nearby. Whose presence might they accept that I could conceivably mimic, as I bobbed along in the pass? I was not sleek and fast like a dolphin, and a sea turtle wouldn't swim in one place as I did.

A great while ago, Caribbean monk seals lived in the Gulf of Mexico. They were fish eaters, never a predator of birds. I wondered if my brown shoulders and dark tank suit, my round head and my fleshy floatable body might register in the genetic memory of the birds as something harmless, like a seal? Of course, none of these oystercatchers would have seen a seal themselves. The last one was sighted in 1952, the year I was born. By gun and by club, monk seals were beaten into extinction, beginning five hundred years ago with the Spanish incursion. The oystercatchers, sharing preferred lagoon and reef habitat with seals, would have borne witness to their massacre.

Lost in thought, I grew careless. The impulse of the waves pushed me toward the shore, until I floated only yards from an oystercatcher standing guard on a low berm while its conspecifics prodded food from the sand. Another of the birds bathed vigorously at the Gulf's edge. Twice he shook water over his back and wings, flapping so hard that he rose off the ground. His thick pink feet climbed the air as if he mounted small steps. The guard bird fixed me with one nervous, startling eye: its chrome orange lid ringed a lemon-yellow iris, all of this color set in ebony head feathers like a jewel in a black velvet box. I had officially been noticed, no longer a benevolent part of the landscape. When I squirmed against the sand, all of a sudden beached, the guard bird seesawed its head and tail. "Wheep! Wheep!" he called, alerting his cohorts. "Time to go! Time to go!" Maybe I resembled an alligator now, or maybe just a human who had ventured too close. Either way, the birds could not tolerate me, and they wheeled away uttering rapid piping calls, flying low to the water.

I ESTIMATED the young birds I had been watching were about four and a half months old, for I had observed pairs of adult oystercatchers bowing and courting, then copulating, when I spent time at the pass in February. Now it was the September equinox. I did not see them build their nest scrapes, but I knew that by April the pairs had chosen remote spots to settle, only a couple of yards from the high water mark. Over the next four weeks, the parents kept potential predators away, and with their warm bodies, they incubated each chick's growth inside its shell, as if they slow-fired a precious ceramic pot. Within each egg, drifting in embryonic fluid, four finlike buds grew into a pair of pink legs and tiny downy wings. Two days before hatching, the egg-bound chicks began to call. Their parents heard the faint peepings and shortened their absences from the nest scrape. When the chicks could be contained no more, when their wings could no longer remain folded, they pipped star-shaped fractures into their shells, flexed their shoulders and cracked free. The brand-new birds tumbled onto the sand and fell into sun glare, the light of the rest of their lives. Unfurling their limbs, aggressively hungry, the newborn oystercatchers scrambled upright and began to navigate a very dangerous world. In thirty-five more days, the young birds would begin to fly.

WHEN THE OUTGOING TIDE drops away from the bars in the bays and lagoons, oystercatchers come alighting. Most of the oysters they consume are small, irregularly shaped "coon" oysters. In the mid-1800s, a Massachusetts taxidermist and bird collector, Charles John Maynard, described how the birds penetrated their prey. "When the bivalves gaped open," he wrote, "the birds would thrust in the point of their hard, flat bills, divide the ligament with which the shells are fastened together, then, having the helpless inhabitant at their mercy, would at once devour it." Maynard continued, "They were not long in making a meal, for specimens which I shot after they had been feeding a short time were so crammed that by simply holding a bird by the legs and shaking it gently the oysters would fall from its mouth."

During the 1980s I often camped with friends on winter weekends on an island north of Cedar Key. At low tide, we would chisel clumps of oysters from the chilly water and drop them in the bottom of our old Grumman canoe. Then we'd knock the oysters apart with hammers, culling out plump singles to eat around the campfire. The smaller ones we'd throw back on the bars to grow.

Winter fog muffled all sound, except for the rasp of our boat on the shell banks. It was a quiet world, until wintering flocks of oystercatchers—hundreds and hundreds of them—whistled through the dusk, veering and parting their companies around our canoes. Our oyster knives matched the chisel-tipped bill of the birds in design and utility, if not color.

AFTER A killing red tide cloaked our coast in the fall of 2005, Jeff and I inventoried the islands from Bald Point to St. Vincent by car and from our powerboat, assessing the damage. It had been five days and ten tides since the unicellular dinoflagellates (*Karenia brevis*) had bloomed in the nearshore waters. The tiny creatures had reproduced in unimaginable numbers, tinting the water brick-red with their bodies. Scales and bones of mullet, flounder, and shark corseted the beaches. Their flesh rotted and sunk into the sand. It looked as if the Gulf had sickened and vomited her own creatures onto the coastal strands. In some places, a burlap of fish skin was all that remained. We tied bandanas over our mouths and noses to try to filter the stench. Even the sky mourned, dragging a great cloud cover over its face. This was no pleasure trip.

At Bald Point, ghost crabs had pulled two or three grunts (or toadfish or puffers) to their burrows, or dug new ones around the corpses. Here was a great bounty of protein, the crabs must have believed. But red tide organisms produce a neurotoxin that affects muscle function and kills many kinds of marine animals. Disoriented and poisoned, the crabs, instead of skittering across the sand, flipped onto their backs and waved their legs feebly as we walked among them. We watched a juvenile eagle feed on a beached mullet on Dog Island and counted seven vultures grouped around an enormous bloody stingray on St. Vincent Point. We wondered if the raptors would survive the toxin that had killed their carrion.

On the bayside of St. Vincent, we listened to the shells of thousands of dying fiddler crabs clink spasmodically along the low tide beach. Hundreds more lay still, already expired in their borrowed homes. On every inbreath, the oily stink of death coated our lungs. We were nauseated, saddened, and afraid.

Watching an oystercatcher die was the worst of that terrible day. I spied it at the end of a spit of land we eponymously call Oystercatcher Point (we nearly always see one there). This bird's wings brushed the ground, like a cape. Its brilliant watermelon bill—slightly parted—was propped against the sand, and dug in at the tip. Its eyes were squeezed into slits of orange pigment, same as the bill. The bird barely breathed, but when it sensed our approach along the beach, it had just enough strength to dilate its pupil and round the orange rim of its eye.

"Let's go now, Jeff," I said. "This is breaking my heart."

Stepping back into the boat, I wept at the oystercatcher's death. Even though it was only one bird on the haunted beach, I was able now to imagine the possibility of its extinction. This is something we rarely see—the end of a line of wild birds. Yet it is happening in our lifetime, as it has before.

THE FIRST great collapse of the planet's birds was set in motion by merchants who, like corporations today, were eager to trade other lives to turn a profit. Colony-nesting birds were targeted and slaughtered for their breeding plumes, their young left to starve. In her essay "The Plumage Bill," Virginia Woolf wrote that "we must imagine innumerable mouths opening and shutting, opening and shutting, until—as no parent bird comes to feed them—the young birds rot where they sit." Oystercatchers lacked the delicate aigrettes (breeding plumes) of the herons and egrets, who were massacred by the millions. But they did not escape the plundering of market gunners and egg collectors. Some milliners even created black bonnets from this shorebird's dark feathers.

I was not yet born when women strolled city streets wearing chapeaux adorned with whole dead birds and their body parts. Nor could my grandmothers have afforded such luxury. But they must have witnessed this excess in New York City, where 83,000 workers turned wild birds into hats—and profit. In 1903, the price offered to hunters was thirty-two dollars per ounce of plume. The feathers were worth about twice their weight in gold.

By 1886 oystercatchers had been completely extinguished from the coastline of New York, and from New Jersey's shore a year later. By the turn of the twentieth century, the variety and abundance of bird life worldwide had been horrifically reduced. How could any finery to decorate our bodies, even any amount of gold to line our bank accounts, justify the slaughter of these sentient beings, these companions?

WITH THE PASSAGE of the Migratory Bird Treaty Act of 1918, most wild birds escaped the guillotine of extinction, although they never returned to their previous numbers. Among the rest, as direct human impact significantly dropped, American oystercatcher populations slowly rebounded in the twentieth century.

But today, oystercatchers are rare and very local in distribution once again, just as they were a hundred years ago. Their feathers are now protected, but the space and privacy they need to live and procreate are not. Like several dozen other shorebirds, American oystercatchers are confined to the very edge of the coast to nest, roost, and overwinter. Their nesting season runs from April to August, which coincides with the peak of human traffic. In earlier days, sheer size and alert defenses enabled adult birds to protect their eggs and young from marauding crows and other predators, but the present-day threats to nestlings are more than the most vigilant parent can fend away. Powerboats, personal watercraft, people and dogs walking and playing—the "feather trade" of the twenty-first century—displace birds from the narrow ribbon of coastline we ought to share. Downy oystercatcher young are nearly invisible, grizzled with a pale pinkish buff protective coloring. In response to a parent's alarm call, the chick will squat in the sand and can often escape detection. Herbert K. Job, an early naturalist, "once hunted thoroughly over a barren strip of sand, where he knew there was a young oyster catcher, without success; he was about to give it up and go away, when he saw a little wisp of driftweed at the water's edge on a strip of bare wet sand; and beside it the young bird was lying, flat on the sand and absolutely motionless. It did not move . . . [until] it was touched . . . [then] . . . off it ran as fast as it could go." But on beaches where trucks are permitted to drive, or dogs and coyotes wander, hunkering down to hide does not protect the birds. On some breeding beaches, 20 to 100 percent of a season's chicks may be killed. Oystercatchers try to adjust to our oblivion by attempting to nest among Australian pines or Brazilian peppers, or on spoil islands, or even on the gravel rooftops of shopping centers. But it remains to be seen if they can survive.

THE OLDEST KNOWN fossil records for oystercatchers appear about 5 million years before the present. Over all those eons, Earth blended and deepened the power and crimson hue of its bill, outfitting the oystercatcher with exactly what it needed to ride the shifting coast. As the violent continents rearranged themselves and the seas rose and fell, the big-billed birds successfully traveled through time in an ageless intercourse with the saltwater edge.

When our ancestors found their way to this shore, a mere ten or twenty thousand years ago, what did the oystercatcher signify to the human—long before, that is, we labeled them a commodity, a source of marketable plume, flesh, or egg? Or ask the question another way: as we look to the future, what do our great-grandchildren stand to lose if we drive the oystercatcher from the beaches and backwaters and leave it behind forever?

I never come to the end of my fascination with oystercatchers. If I cannot comprehend how this bird and all the other wild things are linked to my own survival, and to the web of life that holds us all, at least I can trust this moment of awe when I see one, which throws open my cramped, technologically imprisoned mind.

Then the oystercatcher reveals itself without speech, although if there were words, they might go something like this: "Young child species, human being, will you look at what 5 million years of evolution on this planet has made of me? See how the specificity of living on this edge has elongated my bill, impregnated it with the brilliance of a tangerine dawn, outfitted me to harvest the oyster, yes, but also to express great beauty?" These birds are not objects, but companions, as essential to the spread of the Gulf Coast landscape as the oyster itself. They offer a richness of variation for our eyes and our spirits, as well as an indication of abundance: here, says the oystercatcher, is both solitude and protein, enough for birds and humans alike.

CHAPTER 14

Robbing the River

THE WAKE of a stripped-down oyster boat chugging back to Eastpoint rocked my kayak side to side. I smelled its diesel engine as the skiff moved upwind. Closer to the bridge, dozens more of its kind were anchored over a small stretch of water.

The year was 1994.

As I paddled deeper into the bay toward the oyster boats, my course took me between bobbing rafts of sea ducks, mostly scaup. Their sleek rounded heads glittered green in the sun. I saw common loons, horned grebes, and hooded mergansers as well. Soon all those wintering birds would be headed far north to breed. A big-bodied seabird, its wings spread wide as a white pelican, steered vast spirals over the bay. It was a gannet—not an especially rare bird, but you don't often see them inshore. The bird twisted one more tight circle high in the air and then arrowed into the water. When it resurfaced, the gannet opened its body feathers as if it were an umbrella, and floated on the sound like a giant puffy kernel of popcorn.

I drew my kayak alongside a boat owned by Andy and Michelle Chambers, who were working West Lump Reef, an underwater ridge two miles due south of the tiny town of Apalachicola. The closest human beings were a mile away, laboring at another oyster bar. The sun was warm, the clouds lacy.

Andy Chambers maneuvered his handheld oyster tongs like giant scissors, open and shut, open and shut. His gaze was fixed on the horizon. He was concentrating on the feel of an oyster reef eight feet below the surface. Great tributaries of muscle and vein traced his arms, as he swung the dripping, fourteen-foot rig out of the water and into the air. A half a bushel of bay oysters clattered to the boat's back deck. To my unpracticed eye, Andy Chambers could drop his tongs anywhere in the bay and do just as well as here, but that wasn't true. There was a lot of instinct and experience involved in his trade. Michelle, swathed in a huge rubber apron, broke apart the clusters of mollusks with a heavy cull iron and sorted them by size.

"Today we are after single 'cup' oysters," she told me.

Andy passed me a roughened oyster so I could finger the rounded carapace that half-shell aficionados prefer. Tomorrow or the next day, this oyster and eleven others would fill out a platter anywhere from Miami to Canada.

The whole time we talked, the couple never stopped working. Their story was punctuated by the slap of waves against the hulls of our boats. A light breeze quilted the water's nickel gray surface, and the sun shattered it into a million glittering shards. "This is what I love to do," said Andy Chambers simply. "It means freedom."

THE WARM, mocha bay that rocked the Chamberses' skiff was almost completely embraced by the sheltering arms of St. George and Dog Islands to the east, Little St. George to the south, St. Vincent to the west. For thousands of years, generation after generation of oyster larvae rooted themselves on layers of mature oyster shells, thriving on the nutrients delivered from deep inland. Conditions in Apalachicola Bay were close to perfect for oysters, so perfect that 90 percent of all the oysters produced in Florida, roughly fifteen hundred tons of oyster meat, were harvested here each year. About three-quarters of the nine thousand residents of Franklin County made their living directly from the seafood industry.

Later that day, I visited Florida Shellfish, one of dozens of state-certified processors that crowded the shoreline of tiny Eastpoint and neighboring Apalachicola during the mid-1990s. Even on a Saturday, the warehouse swarmed with workers washing, sorting, shucking, and packing. The back of the building was open to the frothy chop of the Gulf so that oystermen could dock and haul their catch directly inside. In the front room, I watched a worker dump bushel bags of oysters, one after another, through a rotating tumbler. A conveyor belt carried the mollusks the length of the room, where workers separated and graded the shells as small, medium, or select. Then they packed them into boxes and shuttled them into giant coolers to await a Boston-bound freight truck later in the afternoon.

"Like any business involving perishables, this is as hectic as can be," said Brooks Wade, the company's owner, as he led me through a maze of hoses and hand trucks. "It's a very simple industry, but very complex as well. Scheduling is everything and weather is our religion. On pretty days, the oystermen will bring me as many as four hundred bags. When the weather blows I might get fifty."

In the back room, eight women stood at tiny stainless steel workstations. A fine spray of shell and muck dampened the air and the cement floor. Like a giant slot machine, a conveyor belt ground forward and back, dumping mounds of oysters onto each shucker's table. The din was off the charts.

Wade introduced me to Carrie Sapp, a big-boned woman with thick glasses. "This is a no-boss job, the only job I'd have," she said. "But it ain't fun."

Sapp grabbed an oyster and ran its valve against the screeching wheel of a modified bench grinder. Then she inserted an oyster knife into the broken shell, pried it open, and scraped the meat into ice water. Simple. Also monotonous, noisy, and exhausting. An experienced shucker like Sapp could easily clean ten gallons of oysters a day, earning five dollars per gallon, she told me.

"Yesterday I shucked fourteen gallons and finished by 2:30," Sapp said. "I've got me a system."

"She's a champion," said her daughter Liz, working at the next station.

Wade explained that in Eastpoint, you don't tell your employees what to do, you ask them. "And sometimes, you plead with them," he said. "If they take off for a while, you kiss them when they come back. They know we need them more than they need us!"

"This bay has some of the most phenomenally productive oyster reefs in the Western hemisphere," Wade told me before we ended our interview. "Still, ours is a troubled industry." Florida Shellfish went out of business some years ago, but one thousand oystermen and a handful of other dealers and distributors, some going back four generations, have continued to make a living off Apalachicola's oysters.

FOR AS LONG AS oysters have grown in Apalachicola Bay, people have eaten them. The evidence of centuries of enjoyment is in the shell mounds eroding from the back side of the islands. By the 1850s oysters were being packed in barrels and shipped to neighboring states and northern markets. Oyster shells had accumulated on Indian Pass in such quantities that they were plowed without a thought into the first hard-surface roads on that peninsula. "We had worlds of oyster shells out there," remembered lifelong resident James McNeill.

When William Hornaday visited St. Vincent Island with his wife to write a monograph about it in 1905, he said, "But, even if they took all the oysters from these waters—which is fairly impossible—there would still remain that glorious unnavigable bivalve preserve called Oyster Pond, which is well stocked with big succulent oysters, as fine as any that my wife ever ate, which is saying much. . . . Josie Dear is related to the Hae-man-to-pod-i-dae—the oyster catchers; and to give her the time of her life, we camped for two days within striking distance of Oyster Pond. . . . [S]he . . . ate an unearned increment that fairly astonished the natives. Really, the New York oyster is anemic and tame in comparison with the St. Vincent product."

In the 1920s the bivalves were still so plentiful and grew so big that a single mollusk made a meal.

"And if my mother wanted oysters, she asked for three," wrote Charles Marks, who lived with his family on St. Vincent Island as a boy. "We could step out on one of the oyster bars in Big Bayou at low tide and pick up oysters that were a pint apiece. That's all we needed for one sitting, and I never could finish mine it was so big. Naturally they were fried, as nobody wanted a pint of raw oyster in one gulp."

OYSTERS are humble creatures, lacking even the eyes of scallops. Crouched at the merge of salt and fresh, air and water, they open themselves to filter the flow of nutrients. A good Apalachicola oyster fairly brims over its half shell, so undefended that you know your body will absorb it whole. Earthy, quivering, almost sexual, the oyster offers itself to our pleasure.

In late 2013 the Franklin County Seafood Workers Association convened to vote on salvage measures for the industry that was their lifeblood. It was unlike any meeting I'd ever attended. About two hundred oystermen and -women packed the main room in the fire station in Eastpoint. Most wore caps over faces charbroiled by the sun, and all were powerfully muscled.

Exactly at 6 p.m., President Shannon Hartsfield abruptly opened the meeting.

"Let me just kill some rumors," he said. "You all know the river's gone low. It ain't getting better, it's getting worse.

"And y'all know there ain't many oysters. If we take two hundred boats down there, if we all go down there, we will kill it."

The room hissed with discontent. I was listening in on a long-standing conversation, and everyone had an opinion.

"I vote we open the whole fucking bay," a man in a green T-shirt with wild curly hair interrupted.

"You shut up, we cain't hear," yelled a woman behind me.

Hartsfield shouted over the rising clamor. His voice was hoarse with strain. "We can go ahead and destroy what little we have now. But here's what we propose we should do." He laid out a plan for closures of portions of the bay to give young oyster larvae time to root themselves on the reefs and grow into legal size.

Another man jumped to his feet and Hartsfield motioned him to speak.

"We might as well move out of town as close down the bay," he yelled. "I know of two more men this week that got 'hill' jobs."

More tumult ensued. Others stood to talk, in no particular order I could discern. Some had practical ideas, others were just plain mad.

The man sitting on my left apologized to me (an obvious visitor) for the disorder and rancor in the room. "It's just like this when we get together," he told me. "There's going to be a fight or two outside when the meeting is over."

I had noticed people stalking from the room, one or two at a time. I suspected that their anger had more to do with the state of crisis in the bay than with individual disagreements. The lives of Franklin County residents—forty-six hundred households—are as closely tied to the health of the Apalachicola Bay, as oysters are to a reef. Some have stable family and financial networks to help see them through this crisis, but others live in poverty, with significant multiple strikes against them, such as mental health issues, substance abuse problems, or criminal records.

Another incoherent outburst from the man in the green shirt. I was pretty sure he fell into the latter category. A pair of Franklin County sheriffs edged him to the door.

I knew it wasn't all about income, either. These oystermen and their families were frightened about losing a way of life.

"I guess there's nothing else I want to do," said fourth-generation oysterman Toby Dalton several years back. "It's hard work, but you get used to it. I really didn't plan on doing nothing else but this the rest of my life, but the last ten years, I've been scared it ain't going to last. This bay is what we're trying to save. Without this, we'll have to leave our homes."

"WE SAY we live in crisis interrupted by disasters," Joe Taylor, executive director of Franklin's Promise Coalition had told me before the Seafood Workers Association meeting. "If that bay closes, that leaves children without food. The average hourly wage here in the county is only seven dollars and thirty-seven cents an hour, and on top of that, our main industry—oystering—is down by 80 percent."

I asked Joe if he thought people could police themselves out on the bay to save the oyster industry.

"I think it's like this," said Joe, thoughtfully. "If you are on that boat and you have hauled a load of oysters onto your culling board, and most of them are too small, under the three-inch limit, what you decide to do is going to depend on how desperate your circumstances are.

"If you've got decent resources behind you, you will have one answer to the key question: Does this one go back in the bay to make more oysters, or go in my bag, to make me money today? If the bay is your 'bank,' as people down here say, and you are living on the edge of poverty, you probably will make the second call."

THE OYSTER FISHERY'S collapse is the most visible sign yet of Apalachicola Bay's vulnerability in the face of decades of dwindling flow from the Flint and Chattahoochee Rivers that originate north of our state line. For twenty-three years, Georgia, Alabama, and Florida have waged an upstream–downstream water war, with Alabama and Florida coming out on the losing end in the courts.

In 2012 the Apalachicola River reached its lowest level and lingered there for a record nine months. Oystermen could barely find several sacks of oysters a day in the bay, only a fraction of the forty they used to fill. As the number of adult oysters fell, their larvae struggled to mature.

I RECENTLY DREAMED that I came to the bank of the Apalachicola River, and all that remained of the Panhandle's mightiest watercourse was a cracked and muddy channel, a tragedy of epic proportions. A version of my nightmare is coming true for the people and the oysters of Apalachicola Bay. For thousands of years, the river has run to the Gulf, carrying in the green muscle of its body a sweet freshwater flow. How could such a river run dry?

In Florida we blame the mining of the river's water on Atlanta, on that city's concrete explosion of growth, on lawns and golf courses, on the reservoir called Lake Lanier, and on all the ways people can think of to slacken their cultural thirst. Farther south, as it passes through Georgia, people want the river to irrigate field crops and pecan groves, to supply chicken farms and paper mills. When the shrunken river reaches its own bay, its own glorious glittering mouth, it no longer delivers the blend of fresh water needed to grow fish and shrimp and oysters and crabs. But it is not for the creatures' sake alone that Florida sends its governor to parry and fence with the governors of Georgia and Alabama. Our crops are not concrete and cotton, but our claim is the same kind of claim. The oysters of Apalachicola have fallen victim to the tragedy of the commons. We will never succeed in fairly apportioning the flow of the Apalachicola until we advocate not just for crops (including concrete and seafood), but also for the inborn rights of the extraordinarily complex web of life, as well.

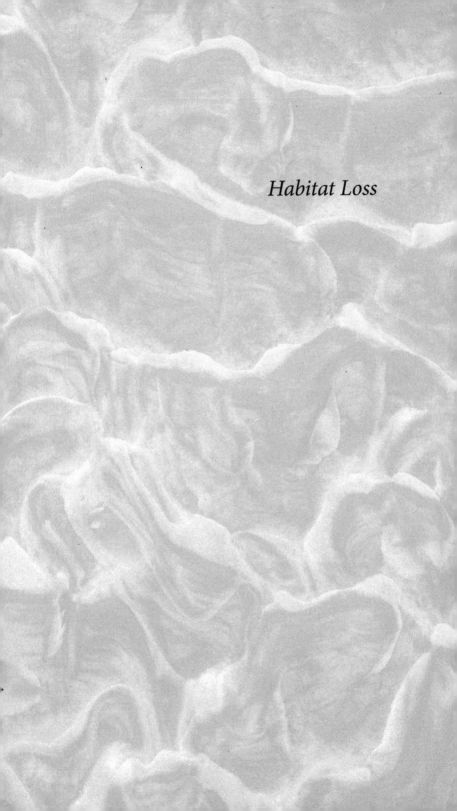

Habitat Loss

CHAPTER 15

Evolution's Larger Concerns *Beach Mice*

"IF YOU COULD just see a St. Andrew beach mouse, you couldn't help but like it," said Dr. Jeff Gore, a longtime friend and colleague.

"Tell me why?" I asked. In all the years I had worked with this scientist, I had never heard him try to make a case for what I would call the "cuteness factor" of a rodent, even an endangered one. Outside the window of the truck, we passed by some of the area's realty agencies: Paradise Coast, Boardwalk, and Beach Realty. We were traveling west on Cape San Blas Road, toward the cape itself.

Jeff handed me a photo from a file folder resting on the seat between us. I studied the image, and I had to concede his point: the tiny animal's eyes glistened like blackberries. Its ears were large, soft, and vulnerable, its fur snowy white. And there was a touching dignity in its stance at the mouth of its sandy, sea-facing burrow.

My friend the scientist is also beautiful, with eyes as clear and azure as the Gulf just beyond the dunes. He is a modest man, and he would never say this about himself, but I am convinced that his efforts to save endangered beach mice engage him squarely in the larger concerns of evolution.

Four subspecies of beach mouse, all isolated from one another by inlets, live on Panhandle barrier islands between St. Joseph Peninsula in Gulf County and Perdido Key in Escambia County. The mouse we are seeking today—the St. Andrew beach mouse— lives between Money Bayou and East Crooked Island. As of 2002, it was reduced to only two small populations, one among the dunes in and near St. Joseph Peninsula State Park and the other centered on East Crooked Island on or near Tyndall Air Force Base.

The St. Andrew beach mouse was listed as endangered in 1998 by the federal government, after scientists were able to show that the small animals had been reduced from their historic distribution by nearly 70 percent. Not surprisingly, their decline tracks the explosion of second-home development on the north Gulf Coast.

To keep these beach mice from going extinct: that is Jeff Gore's goal.

TOURISTS FLOCK to Florida to visit Disney's mouse, even though they know Mickey is a monstrous made-up cartoon. During decades of tracking wild beach mice and watching their populations plummet, Jeff and his colleagues have wondered how to open people's hearts to this subspecies, as they do so freely to the pseudorodent named Mickey. "Beach mice are really cute," Jeff said. "And they do have very snowy fur. So why is an imaginary mouse more lovable than the real deal?"

I first met Dr. Jeff Gore in 1981, when I was assigned to help him count birds and check small mammal traps on a proposed power plant site in Illinois. Our paths have crossed many times since in the state wildlife agency where we both have worked. His is a friendship I treasure. Always humble, he described his current position as "mammal research guy for the state of Florida." For thirty years, Jeff has studied and tried to protect Florida's panthers, bats, bears, beavers—and beach mice.

"My job is to pay attention to all of the signals out there, not just the animals on the brink of extinction," said Jeff. "But how do we establish our priorities? I've only got five employees to cover the whole state.

"Since these beach mice are critically endangered, right now they take more of my time."

TODAY, Jeff planned to spot-check a number of sites on Cape San Blas to answer a simple yes or no question: do St. Andrew beach mice still live here? I had asked if I could come along while he looked for mice and refined a sampling strategy to count them.

"Just remember you won't see the mice themselves," he had said to me over the phone. "Besides being endangered, they are nocturnal and extraordinarily shy."

But I felt happy to help look for their tracks in the blindingly beautiful sand dunes of Cape San Blas, on property owned by Eglin Air Force Base. Beach mice had been gone from this site for many years, but this was the best remaining shot at new habitat. Today we were checking to see if any mice had been able to reoccupy the area.

"Here you've got a record of whatever was moving around last night," Jeff pointed out cotton rat tracks, which he described as "twice as big as a beach mouse's." As we stepped lightly over the fragile dunes, we also spotted the footprints of coyotes, ghost crabs, plovers, foxes, and dogs.

"We will definitely see beach mouse tracks if they are still living here," my old friend told me, cheered by all the animal sign in the sand. "Sand conditions are perfect today."

Jeff explained how he and his colleagues have specially rigged plastic tubes to monitor the animals' populations over time. "Here's how it works," he said. "A strip of thick paper coated on one end with dark ink is carefully inserted into the white PVC tube. Further inside, a pile of sunflower seeds lure the animals. If they accept the bait and enter the tube, the mice will step across the ink pad and leave their black footprints behind for us to tally." The track tubes we would be checking later that day were part of the long-term sampling project initiated by Jeff Gore and others in the mid-1980s.

WE DIDN'T FIND any sign of the beach mice on Eglin, but near the state park, at a small public beach access farther north up the Cape, we got lucky.

"Here we go," said Jeff, showing me a wisp of a trail. We knelt on the fine quartz sand to take a closer look. Mouse tracks—about as big around as a pencil eraser—led us to a burrow on the slope of the dune. I might have thought this an opening dug by a small ghost crab. "You can distinguish between the two because the beach mouse entry hole is domed, not circular," he told me.

The trail showed us that the mouse had hopped along a smooth stretch of sand from one big clump of sea oats to another, probably filling his cheeks and belly with fat golden grain. "Beach mice eat seeds from many dune plants," said Jeff. "Easy to harvest, easy to store in a burrow." The mouse creates a storehouse in its tunnels, a seed bank against hungrier times.

"Now we are obviously within their range," Jeff said. "And this is the right habitat." Even though I couldn't see them, I liked knowing that beach mice lived freely in the dunes where we stood.

Jeff swung his arm wide, encompassing the landscape of tall gorgeous sand ridges. "The mice prefer a little height like this, with open vegetation. It's a narrow, linear habitat, right up against the beach. The swale behind the dunes is not a place they can live. A big overwash or hurricane could wipe them out."

I would love to know what takes place below, within the twists and turns and the dark privacy of the beach mouse's underground world.

"It might not be all that interesting," said Jeff, with a laugh.

But still, I am awed when I think about their long evolution, how any mouse that ignored the light of the growing moon, scuttling over cooled-down dune sand as if moonlight were safer than the sun, that mouse did not leave behind descendents. A great horned owl, largest predator of the night on these islands, would devour such careless mice. Through an infinite number of choices—including decisions to stay hidden or brave the growing moon, a line of beach mice who timed their foraging to the dark of the moon are the hearty animals that have rolled with these dunes into the present.

TWENTY YEARS AGO, when St. Joe peninsula was still lightly developed, beach mice (and all lovers of wide-open spaces) could roam the length of the waterfront dunes. But the Gulf-view dunes that beach mice live on are also the preferred habitat of second-home builders on Northwest Florida's coast.

"And everyone has just cut loose doing whatever they like with their landscapes. Some don't care, but most don't know anything different," said Jeff.

I agreed. "Just like anywhere, it's the unmanicured native plants that hold the dunes in place and offer good habitat for wildlife," I said.

We climbed back into the truck and continued north on the peninsula. The road abruptly curved. We passed over Stump Hole, a narrow constriction of the land where massive granite rocks have been imported to hold back the Gulf—at least for now. The trip became a little a less fun.

"This road can't be maintained forever," said Jeff. "But it sure seems like we are going to try. People want to just keep building, just keep making money. They don't want to take the long view, the geologists' view, and they won't take no for an answer, even from nature."

My friend steered a left turn onto a brief stretch of street named Antiqua, and parked where the gravel gave out. He spread a map scored with mouse-tracking sites on the hood of the truck, trying to pinpoint his sampling location.

This place looked nothing like the pristine habitat we had just visited on Eglin. We had parked in the driveway of a huddle of two-story quadraplexes that ringed a narrow path to the beach. The units were built staggered so that each was afforded a glimpse of the Gulf. I stared at what remained between the rental units and the beach—a single, worn saddleback of sand. You couldn't really call it a dune. A few sea oats had been replanted. The tips of the grasses traced the sand with a calligraphy as delicate as mouse tracks.

"Could beach mice actually live here?" I asked.

"Theoretically, they could," said Jeff, giving my question an even-handed assessment. "The fact that these houses are rental units means there are probably fewer cats hunting the mice. Free-ranging house cats are a huge problem for these mice."

He added, "But look how the ocean is pushing the dunes back."

Those remnant dunes—themselves living entities that must constantly roll and rebuild to survive—were trapped between the Gulf and the houses. Someone had put up low wooden fencing to encourage sand to pile and grow in a fixed line, but these dunes would be shifting back in a natural erosion/storm process—and the beach mice with them—were the houses not here. We both knew that the best protection a beach can have is its own unfettered self, a fact universally acknowledged by geologists. But science is no match for the financial incentives for development on the Florida coast.

"To tell you the truth, there's actually nothing here that offers much hope," said Jeff, rolling up his oversized map. "As beach mouse habitat, this place is just barely hanging on." I held the long cardboard tube as he slid in his papers, like a mouse slipping into its burrow.

Just one lot over, a backhoe and a bulldozer sat idle near the thin front line of dunes.

"I wonder if those guys have obtained a permit that considers the impact of their project on beach mice?" I asked my friend.

"Good question," he replied. "Beach mice and dune habitats receive little attention in Gulf County plans. Developers haven't routinely been informed that they are required to protect those resources.

"The inconsistency between Panhandle counties regarding resource protection is mind boggling," said Jeff. "Walton County, farther west from here, has engaged in mediation, management practices, and even litigation, trying to accommodate both beach mice and developers."

WE CONTINUED driving north toward the state park through a blur of chopped-up habitat. Hundreds of rental houses had been constructed on mostly tiny lots, sliced into squares as if the land were nothing more than a pan of brownies at a bake sale.

Our next stop was a real heartbreaker, a gated subdivision named Hibiscus Beach. It was so easy on the eyes. The rolling white dunes were fully dressed in their natural garments: wind-sculpted scrub oaks and pine, beach rosemary and an abundance of flowering grasses and herbs. I believe our human psyche senses when a thing is aesthetically right and healthy, and that landscape was right. Only two of the enormous houses intended for Hibiscus Beach had been built. Here's how one was advertised: "Gulf front! Exceptional decor! This townhouse has it all." Would potential buyers laugh in our faces if we asked them to consider whether "having it all" includes the full array of natural biodiversity, St. Andrew beach mouse included?

"I've found beach mice regularly, right here," said Jeff. "But that's no comfort anymore. All this land is for sale."

"You could come back any time and find it gone," I replied. "People can keep bulldozing these lots on Cape San Blas, but the houses built here will be deprived of a real location."

After a quiet spell, Jeff picked up again: "You know, a place like this could've started with a master plan, telling homeowners what they could or couldn't do, to keep a front dune habitat—not just mice. You could work with developing a 'beach feel' among the community, stressing how residents could retain butterflies, wild-flowers, sea oats," he added. "At the same time, you'd get the dunes' free storm protection."

But the people who designed the bulk of these subdivisions, it seemed, created developments in a cookie-cutter fashion, for the convenience of people, rather than a comfortable fit with the land.

PERHAPS it's unreasonable to insist that humans care about hard-to-see beach mice, site their homes back a bit farther from the Gulf, and retain the primary dunes. But this mouse stands for more than itself and the unique genome that it has brought forward through the eons. We should protect endangered species because they preserve a singular set of biochemical processes, and it doesn't make sense to obliterate that information before we even understand it.

In a larger sense, the mouse is the dune. By obliterating the "mouse-dunes"—which are also our own front line against the unpredictable Gulf—we not only extinguish the beach mouse, but we hasten the erosion of the islands. The mouse might actually be a measure of what level of development is sustainable for the human race, as well as smaller, voiceless creatures.

Jeff Gore put it this way: "The presence or absence of beach mice offers a good response to the question: do we have a good stable dune environment here?"

It's hard to protect an animal that's so tiny, and a rodent besides. But beach mice have been evolving for thousands of years. They are evolutionarily significant units. To throw them out for no good reason is something we shouldn't be doing. Somewhere you've got to stop—you've got to draw a line in the sand. We may be the last generation of human beings in a position to turn the extinction crisis around and slow the destruction of complex life on Earth.

"I suppose we'd be insane to take this on now," said Jeff. "But you don't get this stuff back."

CHAPTER 16

Counting Christmas Birds

GRAY MUD sucked at my sneakers and frigid water crept up the
legs of my pants as I forged across a sweep of salt marsh adjoining
St. Joe Bay. Out beyond the docks built for boaters, I'd encounter
no other person except my companion, Barbara Stedman, on that
late December day. We were there to see and count the winter
birds. It gave me a great sense of their territory to walk the length
of the true marsh, a mile or more of it.

As I trained my binoculars on the waterscape before me,
I smiled. Lanky great egrets and shorter, lacy snowy egrets stood
among flocks of sickle-billed white ibis and two kinds of pelican.
A dozen species of shorebirds prodded the sandbars, just waiting,
it seemed, to be sorted and summed.

Barbara Stedman had been keeping tabs of birds along this
stretch of North Florida coast for more than thirty years. She
had invited me to join her for the 2009 national Christmas Bird
Count: our charge was to find and tally as many kinds of birds
as possible in the short hours of a single postsolstice day in our
assigned territory. It's a census, but of birds, not people.

And it's a good thing someone has been watching, because since
1967 absolute numbers of common birds have steeply declined.
Some species have nose-dived as much as 80 percent, including
the northern bobwhite (quail). Many—like evening grosbeaks,
meadowlarks, and several kinds of duck—have lost 50 to 70 percent of their population in just four decades. How can we know
what we are losing if we don't know what was there to begin with?

The gawky dance of a rare reddish egret on a distant bar
caught my eye. I felt a jolt of happy adrenaline watching that bird,
wreathed in a chestnut mane of shaggy feathers, spin and jump as

it chased little fish on foot. Over the course of Barbara's long vigil, she had watched the numbers of this spectacular wading bird increase here in St. Joe Bay, and she even knew of several places offshore where they had resumed nesting. But at the turn of the twentieth century, gunners nearly annihilated reddish egrets, seeking their breeding feathers to pluck and sell. Not a single egret could be counted in Florida between 1927 and 1937. Once the murderous hunting was stopped, this species recovered gradually, but their population is still only 10 percent of what it was before 1880. Reddish egrets remain at risk not because they are directly killed anymore, but because they can live only in natural coastal habitats (like this bay), which have been so degraded and fragmented by our human developments. We—the human species—have also blocked and severed their migratory routes and poisoned them and ourselves with a vast array of pollutants.

WHEN I DROVE down to the coast before dawn to meet Barbara for the Christmas Bird Count, she was already three hours into her work. Barbara was one of a small, voluntary cadre of excellent birdwatchers, the best kind of citizen scientist. Along with her husband, Steve, she established the Christmas Bird Count at Port St. Joe in 1976. The count is not a day to linger and admire any one bird. To tally the highest number of different species, you've got to cover as much diversity of habitat as possible.

"IT HASN'T BEEN a spectacular owl morning," she told me, as I shoved my gear into her small green Subaru. She knew, as a fellow birder, that I'd want to know. "The wind is blowing forty-five miles an hour in places, no way to hear a hoot." The likely candidates she might have detected were screech, barred, and great horned owls, but even a barn owl with its heart-shaped face could have been—has been—seen on this count territory in prior years.

One owl we did hear dangled outside Barbara's window, its call contained in a tape recorder fastened to the car by a purple plastic clip.

"Nyaaaaaa ... nyaaaaaaah ..." The descending, disembodied whinny of the screech owl sounded something like a farmyard goat.

"You're going to hear my screech owl going a lot today," Barbara warned. "It's the only way to get the smaller birds to move into view during the winter. The down side is that I've become partially deafened because of using it so much."

My guide shifted into first gear, and we crept through the fields surrounding the Eglin Air Force Base, blasting the tape to scare up songbirds. We counted quantities of yellow-rumped warblers, a few chickadees and titmice, one snipe, three killdeer, thirty fish crows, and at least "fourteen MoDos," (birder shorthand for mourning doves).

"I'm seeing the fewest numbers of birds today ever," Barbara told me.

The asphalt pads and single-lane roads that fingered into the fields and trees beyond the military barracks looked like pretty disturbed habitat to me. Was that the problem?

"No," said Barbara. "Aside from the state park at the end of St. Joe Peninsula, the land protected by this air force base installation actually is more natural than any other piece of nearby coast.

"The rest of Cape San Blas has been killed by greed and the Flood Insurance Act. People can and do build anywhere they want," said Barbara. "And the local politicians have managed to get everything overpriced, just like they did in Apalachicola."

I thought through my own decades visiting San Blas, thirty years or more, about the things I no longer see. During the 1980s, the beaches from the neck of the cape at Stump Pass to the state park on the peninsula's western tip brandished only shining dune and aquamarine Gulf. How quickly it has been diced into dozens of pastel subdivisions with names like Boardwalk, San Blas Plantation or Barrier Dunes, each populated by condos, townhouses, and freestanding multimillion-dollar second homes. The landscape accommodates a large number of vacationing humans, but it no longer offers adequate habitat for many wild birds.

WILD BIRDS are the most real thing I know to praise. They ignite a contradictory vibration in my spirit, of both desire and release, the place where longing is born. A life among wild birds is hopeful: they offer the comfort of their presence, no matter our other preoccupations. Chickadees and Carolina wrens inhabit the yard we share with them in Tallahassee, alongside tufted titmice with their fine peaked foreheads, flaming red cardinals, and several kinds of woodpeckers that ratchet up the trunks of the trees. I do nothing to deserve these daily birds, and yet miraculously, we live out our wordless, parallel lives. I relish the surprise of living among birds, how I might wake on a December morning and find a fist of black vultures roosting on a garden snag. Every year I watch for the first returning migrants of spring: the parula warbler, the great-crested flycatcher, and the swallow-tailed kite. I love knowing that our planet is threaded by the cycling migrations of these birds.

Living in this world, within our salt and bone bodies, we cannot help cherishing the birds this much. They predated the arrival of our species on Earth by more than 1 million years. Their songs were our first music, their call notes the first patterns on our collective human eardrum. They carry a memory of the time when we lived without separation from wildness, under the spread of the sky.

But I grew up so ignorant of the vocabulary of the wild things around me. My siblings and I noticed only those beings that presented themselves despite our ignorance and cultural myopia. Robins, hopping over the grass. A blue jay, fallen from its nest to our patio. A garter snake wriggling out from underneath a rock. Black ants in a line on the cement sidewalk. Nevertheless, free-flying birds abided above and around me all the years of my growing. We lived underneath trees brimming with woodland species. Surely my subconscious noted their songs, and my eyes something of their plumes and habits of flight.

But on summer evenings we did not distinguish between the drone of the insecticide-fogging trucks spreading DDT over mosquitoes and every other living thing in our yards, and the ting-a-ling of the Good Humor man selling ice cream from his white refrigerator truck. These products were brought to us without our request, or our discrimination.

I did not know it, but Rachel Carson was in the thick of her defense of the natural world in a neighboring northeastern state. My father bought me each of Carson's books, until *Silent Spring* was published in 1962. He could not share with me the heartbreak of the deadly rains of poison shaking the songbirds from the very trees under which we lived, nor the knowledge of the thinning of the eggs of the pelican and the eagle, which I had yet to see.

BARBARA STEDMAN and I continued on our rounds, searching for chipping sparrows and the infrequently seen western subspecies of palm warbler (I felt lucky to discern the pumping tail and yellow tail coverts of any palm warbler at all) in the damp, winter-blond fields. "I've always found them here in big bunches," Barbara told me, scanning the brush. But not a one so far that day.

With our binoculars, we swept the utility lines and poles, looking for unusual profiles. Birders know this part of the cape as a "vagrant trap," which means it is attractive to species very rare to these parts, like vermillion and scissor-tailed flycatchers, and western kingbirds. "Even desert migrants like sage thrashers sometimes show up here in winter as they fly along the Gulf Coast," said Barbara.

We took a brief sandwich break under the weak midday sun before we tackled the marshes. The back of Barbara's station wagon was jammed with packaged food and backup birding gear. "I live in the field for weeks sometimes, and I never know when I'll have time to go to a store, so I travel prepared," she told me. She supplemented my meager lunch with peanut butter crackers and cookies for dessert.

The talk between us the whole long day had been about the birds we saw, or ones we didn't and why not. Now, even as we ate, we didn't chat about children or husbands or politics.

And oddly, I realized, we rarely looked each other in the eye.

"I was trained a long time ago that if you're looking any place but where birds might be, you don't see them. I always scan for birds, even while we are talking. It's habitual," said Barbara.

I realized that I had followed her focus on the count so intently that I couldn't have described Barbara herself. So I studied her for a moment, as if she were the rare bird. She was a small woman, beautiful, actually. Her skin was porcelain, her cheeks fired pink by the sun, and blonde hair curled from beneath a purple fleece cap with earflaps. I guessed she might be in her midsixties.

"You know how some people are good at yoga or running or whatever?" Barbara had noticed me stretching my back to compensate for the binoculars' weight on my chest. "Well, I can sense owls before I hear them." This woman was the kind of birder I wanted to be.

"How do you do it?"

"Oh, it's just a matter of sleeping outside as much as possible, listening to the sounds of the night." Barbara spoke carefully, considering her words. Every question I asked about the area's birds, she answered from her own long—and irreplaceable—experience. I felt so grateful that she had invited me along on this Christmas Count. Despite my passion for birds, I feared I would fall into Barbara's "mediocre" category, the moniker she applied to people who watch birds but don't improve their identification skills significantly, year to year.

"Susan," Barbara said seriously, "You've really got to pay attention and learn this Christmas Bird Count territory. Someday I might not be here to do it." I gave her my word.

EVENING THREW its long dark cloak over the once bountiful peninsula of Cape San Blas. We sat in Barbara's car in a tiny park, completing the day's final tally in preparation for the postcount dinner at a Mexican restaurant in Port St. Joe. A sheaf of robins erupted in the yaupon hollies outside the windows of the car.

Barbara had kept a running estimate of those red-breasted beauties in her head all day long. It seemed like they had been everywhere, gobbling gallberries, hopping along the sides of the roads, chuckling among themselves in soft syllables: pup pup pup pup pup.

"Fifteen hundred, that's how many we have seen," she pronounced, looking up at me from her list. That sounded like a great ringing abundance of bird, good news from the winter world of robins. But the count totals as a whole were sobering.

"Numbers are down by any measure this year," said Barbara. "It's almost like there is a plague. I'm only short a little—species-wise—but my total numbers are less than 50 percent of usual. I don't know why things are so absent."

I asked Barbara what she thought might bring back our birds.

"I believe there are only three ways to make a difference for birds," Barbara replied. "Create a database that can stand up in court. Educate people. And create a strong political base." Of these tasks, she had fashioned a lifework on behalf of birds.

Pollution

CHAPTER 17

Stealing the Dark from Sea Turtles

IT'S NOT THE beach houses on St. George Island that bother Bruce Drye when he worries about the nesting of loggerhead sea turtles. What keeps Bruce up at night—because they kill so many endangered baby sea turtles—are the lights. I met up with this sea turtle advocate in the lighthouse parking lot at 5:30 a.m. on a midsummer morning. Over the course of the day, I didn't see a single turtle, but by walking with Bruce, I gained a startling understanding of St. George from the imperiled animal's vantage.

The heavens were still fully dark when I arrived. Or at least they should have been. Even though no business was open so early, the island's tiny downtown radiated a brilliant glow. You could have read a book by it.

"That's the newest contribution to our light pollution," said Bruce, waving at the gift store on the corner of Gorrie Drive and 1st Street. This one establishment, with its repeating banks of interior fluorescents, outdoor stadium lights and glowing ice machine, created a deadly halo of lumens sufficient to disorient beach-nesting sea turtle mothers and their hundreds of hatchlings for many blocks around. I hadn't realized how lethally the lights that make us feel safe, and the spotlit signs that never let us forget, day or night, the names of our churches and gas stations, can disrupt the lives of sea creatures.

We left our vehicles and strode two blocks east past the rental row houses known locally as the "Skinny Minnies," then crossed over to the beach. Bruce lit our path with a flashlight blunted by red, turtle-safe screening. The air was warm and languorous. Without wind to push or pull, the surf folded quietly on the sand. At the high tide mark we began our four-mile survey, checking to see whether new sea turtle nests had been laid during the night. Between the tall beach houses, light blared from the downtown, and slatted shadows on the sand.

"Intended or not, this sky glow is visible five miles down the beach, and our low-hanging coastal humidity further reflects the light," said Bruce. "Every year we have a turtle nest here." He pointed at a flattened stretch of sand in front of a blue Skinny Minnie.

"And every year, two-inch baby hatchling turtles that have just dug out of their sandy nests will walk parallel to the beach and scramble through the alleys between the houses right out to the street, toward the bright downtown lights. They think they are headed to the water. They've evolved over millions of years to aim for the reflective offshore horizon of sea and sky. Our artificial lights aren't something they can adjust to."

Security lights, neon signs, and poorly curtained interior lamps harm turtles in two ways. First, they confuse and alarm the mother turtle crawling from the sea to lay her eggs. Second, sixty days later, the same lights will mislead her hatchlings trying to scurry to the safety of the sea. In 2011, on St. George Island alone, 41 of 143 nests were disoriented due to lighting issues. Statewide, hundreds of thousands of hatchlings die in this way every year.

As we continued our survey, I sensed the sunrise at my back. But I didn't dare turn to look for the slip of the sun, because the morning's venture was not about admiring the dawn. There was an urgent task at hand.

Bruce talked as fast as he walked. "If I get a call, or somehow anticipate a hatch," he said, "I usually end up chasing down a hundred newborns frantically scrambling every which way, into the street or under the houses or into people's chlorinated pools. My federal permit allows me to pick them up and transport them into the Gulf at the state park if they are headed the wrong way. I'm always glad to do it, but it's not a proactive way to protect an endangered species, that's for sure."

The sky brightened and Bruce clicked off his flashlight.

"Keep your eyes open for pairs of linked tracks about three feet apart," said Bruce. "A 'crawl' tells us a female loggerhead, or rarely another species of turtle, emerged onto this beach to nest last night." On the western horizon, mountain ranges of pink clouds reflected the rising sun. Even though it was only seven o'clock in the morning, our clothes were soaked with sweat. Bruce's T-shirt featured (what else?) sea turtles. The ball cap that topped his long gingery curls read "Turtle Volunteer." I glanced at the aquamarine Gulf. A swim would be great about now, I thought to myself, but I knew we had miles to go before we'd finish.

With Bruce setting the pace, we pushed on past the newly reconstructed lighthouse that pointed smooth and white in the air; next, the Buccaneer Inn; then, the Blue Parrot Restaurant. Each facility represented a battle of lights, won or lost for the turtles. The lighthouse, for example, would not be lit during nesting season, thanks to Coast Guard protection. But the restaurant's outdoor lighting would continue, literally, to fire the dark.

"See those tiki torches?" said Bruce, waving a hand at the popular beachside eatery. "We have pleaded with its owner for years, begging him to modify his lights when baby turtles are likely to hatch. But he claims it's 'an ambience thing,' that he's got to have the flaming lights. And for two years in a row, that motel next door—the Buccaneer—has also disoriented hatchlings."

"I've picked up more dead hatchlings than anybody else in Franklin County," Bruce sighed. "I'm a real grumpy person because of what I see. We are not asking people to turn off their lights altogether. We just want them to shield their lights or install turtle-friendly lighting. There's a whole science to that now. It's totally possible."

Last summer, Bruce resorted to babysitting nests laid in the glow of these businesses. After dark, he'd bring a beach chair alongside a nest coming due, and sit close, waiting for the night the sand would pop alive with newborn turtle babies. "If the lights got turned out before they emerged, I could go to bed," said Bruce. "But not before. Believe it or not, I was able to get all of them safely to the water. But there's no way I can sit beside every one of the eighty or more nests laid on this island each summer."

We came upon a nest laid on June 6 (twenty-nine days earlier), according to the sign that marked it. A pair of ghost crab burrows punctured the smooth surface of the sandy square. Bruce squatted on his haunches and ran his fingers through the sand.

"You learn to read with your fingers," he said. "There's a certain texture, a particular kind of soft spot that tells me the nest is still here below."

In just a few weeks, he told me, this bit of beach will erupt one night, and dozens of tiny turtles will claw out of the sand. They'll blink the grit from their eyes, and an ancient instinct will call them to cross the beach to the Gulf. If the lights in the pastel beach houses on the other side of the dune were dimmed, the little animals would have a good chance of making it to the water.

TWO HOURS LATER, at 8th Street, we left the beach, the morning's job complete. We had checked up on every nest laid along this four-mile stretch of St. George Island. I drove with Bruce in his truck to a sprawling two-story condominium development just outside the state park entrance at the island's east end. We walked around the buildings to the cerulean sea. There was hardly a soul on the beach. Only a few fishermen cast their lines into the water.

"I call this 'the projects,'" said Bruce. Crammed with gear, the shore in front of the condo resembled an abandoned, beach-themed garage sale. Two catamarans, a sunfish sailboat, blossoms of neon beach umbrellas, giant plastic tubes, coolers, cushioned lounge chairs and baby cribs, even plastic kiddie pools, littered the sand. The owners of all this paraphernalia must have been indoors, escaping the oven that is the north Florida coast in July. I knew I was baking.

"Now where's that nest?" said Bruce, squinting in the brilliant sun. How could a turtle have even thought of laying her eggs in the midst of this crowded party scene, I wondered? But Bruce knew it was here, had marked it himself on May 25, fifty-one days ago, so he kept hunting. We threaded between a crimson beach umbrella and a blue sit-atop kayak and found the nest way up at the edge of a very small dune, almost lost in a crisscross of railroad vine. A foot or more under the sand, a mother turtle's eggs lay round and ripe and very close to hatching.

Bruce moved on to a second nest in the midst of the mounds of gear. It was easy to find because it was the only four-by-four-foot square of empty sand in front of the condos. Thigh-high plastic pipe strung together with yellow caution tape staked out corners. Black cable ties secured a small sign with "Do Not Disturb" information. The successful hatch of this nest site, surrounded by vacationers' toys, was entirely dependent on the awareness and the goodwill of the beachgoers. One hundred baby turtles lay beneath the sand and would soon be ready, like butterflies in their chrysalises, to unfold into this world.

The phenomenon of leaving so many belongings on the beach—night and day—for a week or two at a time, is relatively new. Guests like to secure their Gulf view for the length of their stay, and Bruce pointed out that not everything is a problem: for example, the slim poles of the shade canopies don't interfere with the turtles' passage. But larger items such as ice chests block the hatchlings' path and make it more likely that they will be ambushed by gulls and crabs.

Bruce and his wife, Rose, working with a small cadre of volunteers, had developed and printed what he calls a "friendly" educational tag, which they tie to beach gear they encounter on their daily surveys. They only labeled the items most liable to trap baby turtles.

"We've seen a reduction in stuff left on the beach because of our tags but some people just get mad. They'll say, 'I paid a good price to rent this house, and I'm entitled to live as I please!'

"But the way I see it, this is my neighborhood," said Bruce. "We attract visitors down for a week or two at a time without ever telling them how to act. I wouldn't care if I didn't care about the turtles." He sighed. "I blame our Tourist Development Council and the residents that live here. They could do right by the turtles, but they won't. The realtors could really make a difference. They could take the lead to be proud of the turtles and insist on light control, if they wanted to."

Even in retirement, Bruce Drye was a park ranger to the core. After he finished his morning surveys, he offered free talks on sea turtles at the St. George Island Fire Department. This particular afternoon, three dozen people filtered into the darkened room, showered, blush-red from the sun, and looking for something to do in the hottest part of the day. Bruce had cleaned up too and wore a tropical shirt and jeans fastened with a turtle belt buckle.

He began by projecting an image of a sea turtle crawling up the beach. She was enormous, even on the screen.

"Sea turtles are Franklin County's oldest visitors. How long do you think they have been coming here?" he asked, directing his question to the children.

A boy about six years old thrust his hand in the air. "About fifty years?" he guessed, thinking up an impossibly large number.

"More like a million," Bruce grinned under his shaggy handlebar mustache. "Longer than we humans have been here, that's for sure! And yet any of you could see a loggerhead turtle while you are here on vacation. In case you do, I'm going to teach you how to watch them the right way.

"The main thing is to give that mother a lot of room. You know, we can choose where we live and where we have our families," Bruce continued. "But sea turtles have no choice. They are programmed to return to the shores where they were born when it's time for them to lay their own eggs."

Next was an image of a giant mother turtle, tears glistening in her eyes, as she deposited ping-pong-sized eggs into the hole she had dug in the sand. The audience stirred and murmured, moved by the awesome animal's task.

"Mother turtles are very shy and cautious," Bruce told us. "If they bump into a chair or a beach umbrella, or encounter a person with a flashlight, they are easily scared back into the water and no eggs will be laid that night.

"Once she does lay her eggs, the turtle packs the hole with hard sand, then throws soft sand over the site with her front flippers. It's a messy process, but seeing a mother turtle covered with sand, trekking back into the water is one of the most wonderful sights in the world!

"Sea turtles don't need our help," Bruce finished, "except in couple of really important ways. We need to turn out our beachfront lights at night and keep stuff that might trip up the baby turtles off the beach."

After the talk, the children clustered around Bruce, full of questions. Their grandparents bought T-shirts, red turtle-safe screens for their flashlights, and tote bags Bruce and his wife had hand sewn to raise money. How much more could one man do?

I LAY AT THE water's edge in the state park. Small waves unreeled from the body of the Gulf, playing out their impetus over my body and against the shore. I imagined what mother sea turtles must see under the best of circumstances—the rounded profile of the shoulders of the dunes against the night sky. Sea oats clothed the mounds of sand, weighted by the dangle of their fleshy seeds. On this beach, the sand grains, smoothed and rounded to soft powdery talc, made for easy digging. And under the sand was the only safe place for hatching or germinating, so that was where plants hid their seed, and turtles, their eggs.

After sunset, I walked late into the night and was reminded of Earth's true roof. The moon was new and the Milky Way was densely palpable, so three-dimensional it seemed that I could reach out and pull that scarf of stars and planets in close. But at home in Tallahassee, I live with the same disruption as the sea turtles. Two streetlights and our neighbors' carport fixture turn dark into light in my own bedroom. The night sky looks as though it has been emptied of stars. A few years ago we installed heavy blinds on each of our windows, because I could not sleep without the dark. But there's more at stake than simply a restless night.

NOT LONG AGO I lay in a yoga class in the final resting pose of the evening, arms and legs extended. Soothing music poured like syrup over the dimly lit room.

"Part of the practice of yoga includes gratitude," the instructor reminded us. "Both for the yoga itself and for your fellow community of practitioners."

My mind strayed to the nine students around me in the studio. Three were women I knew had been treated for breast cancer. Two had undergone double mastectomies; another had had one breast removed, then underwent six months of chemotherapy. Even as I sent each woman loving kindness, my mind skipped to our leafy, lively community. Within two blocks of our house, I could name three more women who have been treated for breast cancer. None of these women was yet sixty years old when she was diagnosed. Breast cancer is not a new disease, but its frequency is increasing, and it is a terrifying adversary. Doctors beat the disease into remission and sometimes cure, with a blunt trifecta of chemo, radiation, and surgery. That's the best we've got so far. The causes of most cancers are as ill defined as the treatments are imprecise.

Scientists believe they have found one of the instigators of breast cancer: nighttime exposure to artificial light. Electric lights—which have only existed for the past 150 years—impair our bodies' natural rhythms and throw off the biological clock that regulates sleep and wakefulness in the human body. As a result, hormone and melatonin levels are disrupted, which can lead to the onset of breast cancer. For sea turtles, humans, and probably most species on Earth, the regular oscillations between darkness and light are essential to biological welfare and a splendid reminder of the turning rhythms of our planet. We are not evolved to cope with ill-designed lighting that is washing out the dark night and radically altering the light levels and rhythms to which we are all adapted.

I know neither sea turtles nor humans can thrive in good health if we continue to erase the difference between night and day.

CHAPTER 18

Standing Watch for Oil

WITH MY RIGHT HAND, I twined gloved fingers with Heidi, a neighbor from my Tallahassee community. On my left I clasped palms with a man who had driven his motorcycle over from Carrabelle. More than 150 of us stood together at Shell Point beach, silently facing the sparkle of the Gulf of Mexico that defines where we live. We were part of the statewide "Hands across the Sand" demonstration against oil drilling in the Gulf of Mexico. BP's Deepwater Horizon oil spill was months away, but collectively, perhaps presciently, we worried about legislative proposals to permit offshore oil and gas exploration in Florida's portion of the Gulf. Using social-network sites, Dave Rauschkolb of Seaside, Florida, arranged groups in almost every city and county along the Gulf coastline to assemble at the beach on February 13, 2010. Almost everyone wore black, to symbolize the potential effects of an oil spill on our sand. As I held hands with my neighbors, I sent fervent prayers for protection out to the saltwater edge of my life.

Soon after the disastrous spill began in April 2010, I stood on the concrete porch of a seafood store in Panacea, watching a man wrap sheets of the *Wakulla News* around two pounds of shrimp and three mullet for our dinner. The floor was slick and shiny from repeated hosing. The people who fetched the fish out of the big walk-in cooler, gutting, scaling, and fileting as customers requested, wore white rubber boots to keep their feet dry and warm.

A black woman wearing a flowery sweatshirt came up the steps behind me, taking her place in line.

"My heart is just breaking over this oil," she said to all of us on the porch, referring to the travesty that now threatened the whole of the Gulf of Mexico. She held her hands over her heart. "I want some seafood before the oil comes ashore." Behind the lenses of her glasses, I could see her eyes brim with tears, and I nodded my head in understanding. That's exactly why I was here as well.

The woman paused. She turned away to wipe her face.
"I was born in St. Mark's," she continued. "And I've always lived in Wakulla County. My heart is truly breaking." The woman was slight and strong, with narrow shoulders and thick curly black hair. She didn't know any of us, and it didn't matter. She was expressing the contents of all our hearts.

But the store owner broke the mood, lighting into a rant about the government's role in the disaster.

"I can't get any information on TV, radio, or newspapers about the spill," he shouted. "There hasn't been such a cover-up by the federal government in decades." From past visits, I knew this man's politics ran far to the right. His anger forced each of us back into our own solitary experience of the horrific spill.

All summer long, 200 million gallons of crude oil and unknown quantities of toxic dispersant devastated huge expanses of shoreline in the western Gulf. Jeff and I watched for signs of oil, never knowing which visit might be our last goodbye to the coast as we had known it. In the hot months, we normally escaped to cool spring-fed rivers or backpacked in the Rocky Mountains. Not that year. It didn't seem fair to leave. We organized book readings and scientific lectures, we took part in demonstrations and letter-writing parties to our legislature. We walked at St. Marks and Alligator Point, unable to imagine oil coating the emerald marsh grasses, the white sands, or brown pelicans, but needing to be there in case it did. On Mother's Day, we knew many more families going down to St. George Island than staying in town doing brunch. Whether you live in Tallahassee or Crawfordville or Monticello, you consider this your coast, and it is. One mile or forty miles from the saltwater, our homes are built on ancient Gulf shorelines, where one day the sea will return.

On an evening in July, we drove to Wakulla Beach, even though the temperature was 96 degrees when we left Tallahassee after supper, and the air was clogged to capacity with humidity.

"We will probably only be able to stay a few minutes," I said to Jeff, eyeing the threatening cumulus clouds bearing down from the east. "Either it is going to pour, or the no-see-ums will chew us to bits!"

"Let's give it a try," said my husband. So we slid into water shoes and struck out down a path through the marsh grasses toward a tiny tidal creek. Our feet made squishing sounds in the saturated mud. We'd have walked barefoot but for the knives of oyster shells hidden beneath the surface. Under the long-sleeved shirt I wore for bug protection, sweat trickled between my shoulder blades. But I was so glad to breathe in the fecund fragrance of the marsh, and I admired how a vast low tide, intensified by the pull of the new moon, had dragged the water far out in the Gulf, exposing the wide corrugated bay bottom. Normally submerged sea grasses lay limp on the surface of the mud. All kinds of sucking and bubbling sounds emerged from the subsurface, where industrious worms and mollusks were processing the rich nutrients of the tidal marsh into their own flesh.

Battalions of tiny fiddler crabs surged out of the path in front of us. They resembled little families, and their feet were so light it seemed the wind was blowing them across the damp salty sand. Dark rails flittered through the marsh grass, clapping their noisy alarms.

When we reached the creek, the water was tea colored but clear, and still knee-deep despite the outgoing tide.

"Let's get in!" I said, and we pulled off our shorts, easing down into the flow. We sat up to our waists, relaxing against the sand. Cool water ran over our skin. The current supported us as if it were the back of a chair, holding us upright in the creek. Schools of killifish rippled the surface and even bumped against our backs. If a stingray were to swim past, we would have seen it, and the blue crabs kept their distance, so there was nothing to fear.

Two dolphins thrashed in the channel straight across from us, fishing. They plowed through water so shallow their dorsal fins reflected the pastel rays of the lowering sun. I saw glints of small fish thrown out of the water as the dolphins beat their tails on the water's surface.

The sweat washed off our bodies, and our cores began to cool. We were so happy, sitting side by side in that place. All was beautiful. All seemed well. But whether the BP oil disbursed here and coated this abundant landscape with death depended on the winds of summer and the unknowable currents of the Gulf. And over those, we humans had no control. My thoughts began to spiral into dark scenarios.

With effort, I wrenched my mind back to the present perfect moment, to the fiddler crabs just an arm's length away, by the hundreds of thousands. I reminded myself how grateful I was to be there, submerged in the still intact vista I loved so well. My eyes regarded the marsh from the height where my shins would normally be. I could listen to the crabs clicking through the lime-green marsh grasses, an endless forest from a crab's eye view, and I could closely observe what they were doing. And as long as I didn't move, save for the gentle rocking of my body in the tide, they were unconcerned about my presence. Each crab had a mark painted on its shell, resembling a wingspread butterfly, or perhaps a map of the North American continent. The animals traveled by scuttling sideways, each on eight legs, always sideways. The males sported one swollen overgrown claw to signal to potential mates and spar with their legions of rivals, and a second claw of normal size, for feeding. I smiled, thinking of how our friend "Doc" Bill Herrnkind described the function of the major appendage—"Hey, baby, check out the size of my claw!"

The wind blew steadily from the west. On the breeze, we smelled wood smoke that rose from a controlled burn in the St.

Marks National Wildlife Refuge. I feared that west wind now and the vagaries of the summer weather patterns. Along the same Gulf, especially in Mississippi and Louisiana, economies were crashing. We heard that people were suffering from the "tar flu," far worse than a virus, poison to skin and liver and lungs and brain. The economies of the wild things were crashing as well. Uncounted pelicans and gannets and terns, in their ancient practice of hurtling from sky to sea to fish, were dying every day in the oil. On television, we watched dragonflies glued by oil to the tips of marsh grasses, and egrets unable to lift their perfect golden feet from the tarry sands.

Would the oil travel all the long miles from Louisiana to our place before the runaway well could be capped?

The click and mutter of the fiddler crabs returned me again to the present. They sounded like dry seed pods, shaken. I watched them climb the bases of the grasses, grooming them clean, sometimes three or four on a single grass "tree." Even the males—balancing their big hyper claws—did some climbing. They stripped the algae from the grass leaves, sometimes ingesting whole thin strings of it, like spaghetti noodles. Because the females have two small claws, they were able to pick and eat, two-fisted, at twice the rate of the males. Others sorted sediment through their mouthparts, extracted what was edible, and then spit out tiny clean white balls of sand. The crabs were cleaning the marsh!

As the sun fell against the horizon, we stood, toweled dry our legs, and walked back along the narrow path to our car. The slope of shore into Gulf is so very subtle at Wakulla Beach that at low tide, the fiddler crabs forged far out toward the horizon. Claw by claw, they chained themselves together in bold skeins, hundreds and hundreds of thousands of them, their shells pinking in the last of the light. I thought they were creating their own crab version of "Hands across the Sand." Clicking their claws to the new moon sky, they ventured far out over the flats, connected to one another in long jostling stringers, with inherited, rhythmic purpose. They did not expect the oil. They had an aspiration both grand and simple in their movements and their living. As I walked, I could see along the curve of the coast all the way to the vertical white picket of the St. Mark's lighthouse. Mimicking the searching eye of that beacon, smaller sentinels—great egrets—were dotted in an unending chain, like we ourselves, also standing watch.

POSTSCRIPT: The oil did not reach our coast, but more than a thousand miles of shoreline in Louisiana, Mississippi, Alabama, and West Florida were devastated by the spill, including coastal wetlands just like ours. Unprecedented numbers of dolphins and sea turtles were killed directly by the oil, and as they consumed contaminated prey. Recovery of the marine ecosystems in the affected areas will take decades, if it is even possible at all.

Climate Change and Sea Level Rise

CHAPTER 19

"The Shore, Being of Shifting Sand"

A BURNING BELLY of high pressure squatted over north Florida, incubating daily highs of 105 degrees and more. If we had been home in Tallahassee, we might have ducked from one air-conditioned space to another all day long, but instead we were spinning in our boat from the Lanark ramp to Dog Island, easternmost in our barrier chain. With us was our neighbor and colleague, Dr. Cheryl Ward, an archaeologist who specialized in underwater sites. Our destination was the remnants of a lighthouse that once stood in the center of Dog Island. There, I hoped we would piece together a clearer picture of our coast as a landscape in motion.

We flew through Middle Pass along the island's east end, which is mostly owned by the Nature Conservancy and is mostly uninhabited.

"This part of the island is gaining sand and getting longer at a rate of about eleven feet per year," yelled Jeff over the roar of the motor.

Cheryl nodded. "You just can't argue with a barrier island," she said. "It's going to go where it's going to go." I listened to their facts and recitations, and I believed them, but I couldn't see it yet.

The Gulf was a palette of sapphires. A single dolphin fell in beside our boat, its long gray body shimmering in the transparent sea. You almost could have mistaken the animal for the shadow of a cloud except that every minute or so, it gulped air at the surface and then resumed its gallop alongside our boat.

Jeff positioned the boat according to Cheryl's GPS coordinates, and I unfurled the red bimini shade and snugged the anchor into the sand bottom. We peered over the side of the boat.

"This was the final of a trio of lighthouses built in the 1800s to guide boats through West Pass to Apalachicola," said Cheryl,

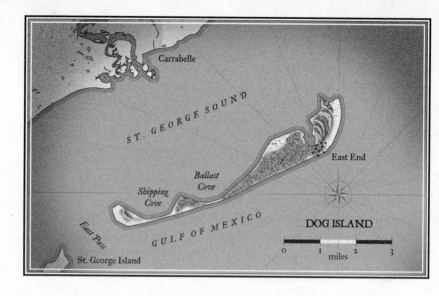

a strong-boned woman with honey-colored hair and skin. "This last tower fell in a single swoop and cracked open like an egg in the September hurricane of 1873. The storm bulldozed the lighthouse keeper's home into the sea as well." Even though the water was spring clear, you could have mistaken the remains of the old building fifteen feet beneath us for a dark bed of sea grass. No wonder this site was so little known.

Dog's shoreline looked to be just a swimming pool's length away, but Cheryl said we were nearly a mile from the beach.

"I can't believe it's that far," I said, squinting at the rim of dazzling sand. "Let's verify it with the GPS when we go in for lunch."

Cheryl stripped off the full-length patterned gauze skirt and long-sleeved blouse she wore over her bathing suit for sun protection. We squeezed our feet into black rubber flippers and slipped over the side of the boat. The water was so smooth, I felt as if I was sliding my body into a silken glove. I adjusted my mask and began to breathe through my snorkel. Following Cheryl's lead, we swam over the lighthouse's body, a drowned tumble of 150-year-old masonry.

Sand perch and sheepshead, striped yellow and black, wound through the wreckage. Stone crabs scuttled where people once tended the light. The ruined beacon was still useful, but as a sheltering reef, not a guidepost.

We breaststroked over the field of debris, startling up a nervous school of baitfish. Large sections of articulated brick masonry lay inert; their position on the seafloor correlated roughly to the original brick tower. A thin layer of silt and periphyton covered the whole, like a dusty old cape. When we came up for a breather, we stood tiptoe, balancing on a section of hollow wall that rose about six feet off the bottom. Our heads and shoulders were in the air, our bodies underwater. I tilted my chin up and sculled with my arms to maintain my footing, breathing hard.

"How did you ever locate this site?" I asked Cheryl, as I disentangled my mask from my hair and shook it clear of salt water.

"I was conducting a survey of shipwrecks around Dog Island with my crew in 1999, using a nineteenth-century nautical chart and sonar imaging to guide us," Cheryl explained. "This lighthouse was a real find. But the summer I surveyed here with my students, we never once saw the lighthouse remains as clearly as we're seeing them today."

Cheryl was eager to take advantage of the translucent water. "Let's go down again and I'll show you the bricks. You can still see how each row was offset from the next to strengthen the tower. It's amazing." We slid back underwater and dove down close, kicking above a brick ridge in the inner tower that once supported a wooden floor or stairway, or perhaps a windowsill.

Cheryl gestured at the remains of lighthouse keepers' quarters lying just to the north, toward the shore. We swam the length of a hollow iron column studded with anemones and bryozoans. The sea creatures waved in the current like Spanish moss in the wind. A century and a half ago, this post raised the home of the Dog Island lighthouse keepers six feet above the sandy shore, well out of range of the surf.

As I treaded water, the tips of my flippers grazed the concrete wreckage. It appeared that the structure itself had slid out into the Gulf, but in truth, it was the island that was rolling as a whole, toward the mainland. We tend to think of storms and hurricanes as destroyers and the coastline as fragile, but undeveloped beaches left to their own devices survive rises in sea level by cycling toward higher ground. Barrier islands will migrate toward the land, keeping pace with the rising sea, and beaches will always be at the shoreline in some form, although in different locations over time. And populations of creatures that live along those shores undulate back with the beach, as changes in sea level transpire—if we let them.

The way it happens is this: during periods of relatively calm weather, sand is transported from offshore to the beach face, which gradually steepens, both above and below the tide line. Then, when a powerful storm blows ashore, the beach flattens itself, acting like a shock absorber and changing its shape as it dissipates the high-energy pounding of the waves. Sand is transported from the upper beach and the dunes to the lower beach, or back offshore.

So what might look like a whole lot of beach erosion is a simple rearrangement of sand, a response to the laws of physics. It's helpful to try to understand the beach as it defines itself, not as a static ribbon of sand and dune that we want to play on. Beaches thrive when they are allowed to act as active margins, rearranging themselves in response to storms and the wave energy that reaches them.

Barrier islands want the same thing as we do. They aspire to stay above the sea. They adjust to hurricanes, to changes in sea level or sediment supply by rebuilding and shifting landward. To save its own life, Dog is backing away from the Gulf.

SEA LEVEL RISES when the balance between water stored on land and water stored in the oceans is changed. It works like this: human emissions of carbon dioxide and other greenhouse gases cause warming that thaws some of the planet's ice. Shrinking mountain glaciers and, even more critically, the melting of the vast ice fields of Greenland are swelling the oceans, which jeopardizes low-elevation coastal areas like our own. Melting ice leaves behind open seas that absorb about 80 percent more solar radiation than frozen water does. And so as the sun heats the ocean, even more ice melts, in a devastating feedback loop. The Earth, not any political or economic system, will be the ultimate arbiter of sea level.

Nearly all scientists, climate experts, and progressive national governments now agree that 350 parts per million (ppm) is the safe upper limit of carbon dioxide in the atmosphere for ourselves and our planet.

But as of 2014, our atmosphere contains more than 400 ppm carbon dioxide, and this number is rising by about 2 ppm every year. For the Earth, this is an unprecedented rate of change, about ten thousand years worth of change compressed into one hundred years. There is more carbon dioxide in our air right now than at any time since humans evolved, more than at any time over the last million years! The Earth is used to slow changes, not fast ones. Gentle shifts allow the biosphere and the planet's species time to adjust. Quick alterations cause biological chaos and disrupt agricultural production. The last time the Earth warmed two or three degrees Celsius—which is where we're headed—glaciers melted and sea levels rose by tens of meters, something that will shake every aspect of human endeavor should it happen again. For the shallow coastline of North Florida, such a rise will mean that the rate of sea level change will not allow the marshes and the islands to simply roll back. In-place drowning and significant overstepping of our current shoreline is more likely.

Along the shoreline of Apalachicola Bay, dozens of miniature scarps ascend the subtle slope of the sand at low tide. They remind me of the results of an electrocardiogram, a medical test that translates the heart's electrical activity onto paper. Scrawling up the beach face as they do, each line marks a moment, a heartbeat, when the retreating water paused long enough to deposit a fraction of a millimeter of sand. Here and there the ribboning bands overlap one another, and then it appears as if someone had taken this beach and squeezed it, so that tiny runnels drain the water back into the Gulf.

But the sand's intricate record will be wiped clean with the next high tide. The only way I can reliably estimate the true edge of the sea is where a deeply rooted tree has drowned. The heart of that pine, a dense furrowed finger of wood, marks where a living thing has gambled on a stationary sea level and lost. We humans are so like that pine tree, throwing our seed, building our homes and our roads right up to the impermanent edge, and hoping for the best.

Underneath our apparently solid lives, below asphalt roads and concrete foundations, we perch atop a rim of sand laid down by the rise and fall of the sea. From the dry sand hills south of Tallahassee, the coastal plain extends thirty miles to the present-day beaches and islands, and then far out across the drowned continental shelf under the Gulf. Salt water has shaped every bit of its face. The Gulf has paused to take a stand at many places between the Cody Scarp and the deep continental shelf over the eons.

When you drive west on Highway 98, beyond Panacea and St. Teresa, where the spiring pines give way to white strand, you may spot a simple green sign at the edge of the road: Gulf Terrace, it reads. No quickie mart or even a gas station marks a town. On your left is open water, and Dog Island, beyond. Gulf Terrace is an edge, one of many ancient shorelines of the Gulf of Mexico, and we ride it, now, in our lifetimes. But in no way is it permanent.

Better that we think of the Gulf Coast as an elastic ribbon of the particular, expanding and contracting at the bidding of the ages of ice. Better to remember that every latitude of this pan-handle landscape has taken a turn at being the breaking edge. Best to keep in mind that the islands we so love are young and fast moving, married to planetary forces of ocean, wind, and melting glacier, because Earth's weather is changing.

If you've been watching our coast over the past decade, you've noticed that the beaches are already sliding out from under the forested edge of the land at Alligator Point, Turkey Point, Cape St. George, portions of St. Vincent Island, Highway 98 between Eastpoint and Carrabelle. But nowhere are the powers of erosion and the rise of the sea as dramatic as at Cape San Blas.

ON A HOT AFTERNOON in October 2012, I swung by the Cape San Blas lighthouse, hoping to find lighthouse keeper Beverly Mount-Douds in her gift shop. Beverly entered the doorway behind me, round cheeks reddened with the effort of climbing stairs. Her breath came in audible gasps.

"Give me just a minute," she said, lowering carefully into her chair. "I've got chronic pulmonary disease. But that's not the worst of it," she continued. "They are closing us down because the land is washing away. I've got to get this whole place packed up and moved in the next five days."

Beverly Douds, who describes herself as a fanatical genealogist and historian, was referring to the contents of two historic keepers' cottages and a century-old brick oil storage building. She had just learned that the land had been declared surplus by the air force and would be soon offered to the private sector for sale.

"I don't want to lose the lighthouse. I want to stay with it," she said.

The keeper was practically in tears.

"Oh honey," she said, "I've got a lot of stories still to share about it. I start getting mad when they get rid of history. But I guess there's no choice since this land is going out to sea."

Tourists in pairs and threes wandered around the small gift shop, chipping in to Beverly's effort to save the historical lighthouse structures by purchasing key rings, Christmas ornaments, locally harvested tupelo honey and commemorative posters.

The poster showed the graphic problem: following the action of waves generated by Hurricane Isaac in August 2012, the lighthouse complex is losing footing, more each day. Only thirty-five or forty feet remain on the south end, and maybe fifty feet on the north end of the beach fronting the old keepers' quarters.

Of all capricious coastal landforms, capes like San Blas are the most unstable. This landscape feature projects into the Gulf of Mexico like the crook of a bony elbow from the giant flexed arm of the St. Joseph Peninsula and is considered one of the most rapidly eroding shorelines in the state of Florida, shrinking an average of twenty-five feet every year.

To warn mariners traveling between the Dry Tortugas and New Orleans about the dangerous shoals extending off the cape into the Gulf, a conical brick-tower lighthouse was first erected here in 1849. A storm destroyed that structure just two years later, but a new one was rebuilt and resumed operation in 1865.

Ten years later, the Lighthouse Board reported: "The base of the tower is very nearly at the same level of the sea, which is but little more than 150 feet distant, the shore being of shifting sand. In a violent hurricane, it is feared, the tower may be undermined." And indeed, by 1882 the second lighthouse was covered by eight feet of water.

I placed my small purchases on the counter, and Beverly wrote me up a receipt on an old-fashioned pad. With her left hand she answered the phone when it rang, cradling it against her shoulder. She told her caller, "We've got cardboard boxes and plenty of newspaper. Just help me get the word out, then come help me pack it all up." Behind her silver-framed glasses, I saw tears in her eyes.

She flapped her hand in a distracted wave as I walked out the door and said, "Work just won't be the same, wherever I end up, without the lighthouse out here behind me."

JUST A FEW hundred feet south of the lighthouse stands a ghost forest, a boneyard like the one we often visit on St. Vincent Island. Fifteen years ago, Jeff and I came across this stressed landscape as we rode fat-tired bicycles along the sand. Many cabbage palms had been simply uprooted or buried halfway up their trunks. Dozens of dead pine trees sprinkled the beach, creating a slalom course for our bikes. I stopped to contemplate the thrown-down bodies of the trees. It looked as if giant darts had been hurled into the sand from somewhere in space. That fanciful scenario was almost easier to believe than that a green living forest had recently stood on this spot.

"And not long ago at all," Jeff said, swallowing some water from an orange Nalgene bottle. "This is a terrestrial environment in retreat. You can see how the beach is literally rolling over the woods. These trees stumps are remnants of a forest that once stood well back from the shore. They are certain evidence of severe erosion."

We stopped to investigate what appeared to be dark soil at the edge of the surf. It was fibrous peat, and it felt more like a potting medium you might plant ferns in than a Florida beach substrate. Small warm wavelets surged around our legs, refilling the depressions in the peat. Several gray, quarter-sized sand fleas circled, unable to penetrate the mire as they would their natural sand habitat. Both the animals and I knew something was very wrong.

Further along, a storm had thrown long fingers of sand into the marshes behind the dunes. "This used to be salt marsh, not beach," said Jeff, pointing. Just beyond the narrow strand, across the island's main road, we could see stretches of grassy marsh. Those, too, were destined to drown, as the St. Joe Peninsula steadily moves toward the mainland.

We wandered around the foundation of a long, low building that hung out over the high-tide line, its pilings aslant, its existence tenuous. When the next hurricane came, that old military structure would go the way of the salt marsh and pine forest.

WEST OF THE LIGHTHOUSE lies Stump Hole. The Gulf gnaws at this thinned-out part of the peninsula, longing to create an island, a new untethered entity, a barrier named St. Joseph, like St. Vincent and St. George to the east. In 1995 Hurricane Opal, one of the most destructive storms ever to impact the coastal zone of Florida, did just that, breaking through here at Stump Hole.

Along this mile or so stretch, an enormous revetment has been built and rebuilt in recent years, in hopes of stabilizing what in the long run can never be fixed in one place. When you drive along County Road 30-E, past the lighthouse entrance onto the cape proper, you know that this is war. Thousands of enormous granite boulders, called "armor rocks" by engineers, have been trucked in from somewhere far to the north to form a long, curving dike.

You cannot blame us as a species of animal, in a certain way, for trying to hold onto what we think is ours, including road access to a lucrative stretch of real estate, or a sandy beachfront lot we purchased and built a cottage (or an enormous mansion) upon. Of course we want to protect our investment. And yet, it's only in the last hundred years that our technological cleverness and powerful machinery have allowed us to try to hold fast to a configuration of coast that has never held stable—ever.

Cape San Blas is so exposed and so vulnerable that homeowners can't even get insurance from the National Flood Insurance Program, although they can buy and build and purchase their own coverage. Private insurance for a beach house with a $1 million mortgage here could cost $30,000 a year.

To protect those big-ticket homes, in the spring of 2009, a nearly $22-million-dollar beach restoration project was completed along seven and a half miles of coast north of the most dramatic erosion area just west of Stump Hole. In another seven to ten years, experts say, the beach will have to be replenished. Restoring one mile of beach costs between $2 million and $3 million. It's a perpetual process that some people liken to road maintenance. But the construction of artificial beaches involves pumping in dredged sand from an underwater source or trucking it to the beach. The environmental cost of such "nourishment" is high. The dredges suck up and crush sea turtles and other creatures living along the beach face. These life forms may recover their populations slowly, only to be destroyed by the next sand pumping. But protection of buildings, not natural beaches, is the underlying goal of most renourishment.

Between the Cape San Blas lighthouse and the heavily armored revetment at Stump Hole, a pair of bald eagles holds a territory in the remaining patch of coastal forest. On the 2010 Christmas Bird Count, my birding mentor, Barbara Stedman, and I walked the beach, climbing up and over dozens of pines knocked into the surf.

"Look!" said Barbara, pointing at the male of the pair, as he delivered a long tail of Spanish moss to build up the nest.

"We are looking at new construction," Barbara told me. "This eagle pair has lost three nests in three years to hurricanes or high autumn tides pulling down the pines as this beach erodes."

We watched the eagle land heavily on a branch just above its massive aerie.

"This nest," said Barbara, "is very temporary lodging."

Unlike the eagle, born into the cycles of this place, which rebuilds its nest on the same stretch of Stump Pass real estate year after catastrophic year, we humans have a choice about how to respond to coastal erosion.

Here are our options. Armor the beach by expensively and fruitlessly constructing hard lines in the sand. Renourish, another costly and ultimately, destructive choice. Or most difficult of all, find our way to graceful retreat in the face of the surely rising sea.

Sand Envy

ROSANNE WOOD didn't know about the lighthouse ruins stranded a mile offshore when she bought a lot on Dog Island in the mid-1990s. But if that beacon still stood you would be able to see it from the third-story deck of the vacation home she built and named Rosi's Roost.

I gripped the deck rail as a powerful east wind set the house aquiver, carrying Forster's terns swiftly down the beach. I rarely had a chance to look down on the silvery backs of these birds.

"I'd always dreamed of having a beach house," Rosi mused as we gazed over the limitless water. Her house fronted on white sand beach and aquamarine Gulf: lovely, lovely, lovely.

"I grew up in Belle Glade in South Florida. The land had all been drained there, converted to sugar cane and vegetables. When I saw all this wildness, I knew this was where I wanted to be."

Far below, a single willet probed the edge of the surf, which wasn't the gradual incline you'd expect. Rather, it chopped off abruptly, ending in a three-inch scarp. When an incoming wave chased the bird up the sand, she had to flap her wings to hop above the rush of water. The willet's plight captured my attention. The whole landscape, I thought, seemed truncated, lacking a necessary sweep. The Gulf was biting off the beach.

Rosi and I descended the wooden stairs to the second story porch, and rejoined our friend Nina in the shade.

"How has the beach changed since you've owned this property?" I asked. Rosi poured me a glass of white wine, and we settled in to talk.

"Every time I come out here, there's less of it," Rosi replied. "We especially miss the thirty-five-foot-tall primary dune we built this house behind. It was seventeen feet wide, as well. It seemed impossible at the time we chose our site, that something that big would just wash away."

Now I could see it, too—the old dune's disappearing footprint, just a shadow on the surface of the sand between where we sat, and the sea.

"When my husband, Pete, and I built this house, our dream house, we wanted to be as close to the water as we could. At that time, the edge of the Gulf was at least seventy-five feet farther out from where we sit today. Our friends warned us: 'Wherever you are thinking about building on your lot, move back twenty feet!'

"I didn't, but I wish I had," she mused, fingering the stem of her glass. "I got my view, but as a consequence, my house will go into the water. Since I've been here, I've seen four houses destroyed by storm surge on this stretch of beach alone."

Rosanne tilted back in her chair and scrutinized the hurricane clips securing her porch roof. They appeared to be rusting. But if anything went wrong with the house, Rosi would be on top of it.

"I'm the 'Mr. Fix-It' in my family," she laughed. Her smile was generous and wide. Her blonde curls were tucked under an orange visor. Even at the beach, she wore long dangled earrings, and her nails were painted crimson. She didn't look the part of a handyman. "But I am," she said. "I enjoy working on the house a lot."

"It's true," added our friend Nina, who had visited here with Rosi many times over the past fifteen years. "The price of admission to the Roost is that you help out with the repairs that constantly plague an island house." That afternoon, Rosanne wanted to replace some torn screen on a side porch, while Nina cleaned the shower stalls in the bathrooms.

"I am a fixer, a problem-solver." Rosi was emphatic. "That is what I do." For thirty-five years, Wood served as principal of Tallahassee's alternative high school. There, she cleared a path and created a supportive environment for hundreds of students who couldn't find a fit in traditional schools. She's got a fan base of grateful parents and young people to prove it.

One friend put it this way: "Rosanne saved my life—and many others—by offering a much bigger vision of what we could be, and helping us all along the way."

"The job of being a principal I could do, and I loved it," Wood agreed. "But out here?" She gestured at the Gulf. "I have a house in the most beautiful place in the world, and there's not a damn thing I can do to protect it. I can keep it clean, patch it up, but, ultimately, I am helpless. There isn't a thing I can do to hold back the Gulf from my house."

IN THE EVENING we walked toward the lowering sun. A sand road skirted the beach. Telephone poles provided an impossibly fragile umbilicus to the few houses still standing along Dog Island's West End.

I remembered visiting a house on this part of the island owned by a prominent Tallahassee attorney. It was more than twenty-five years ago, but the particular stretch of landscape felt familiar. "Do you know where the Haben house is?" I asked. Rosi pointed to a single pipe crusted with barnacles. It stood knee-high, lapped by low-tide waves.

"That's all that is left of it," she said. I was astounded.

A few hundred feet farther along, Rosi waved her hand at a cluster of five cottages perched on tall pilings. "Only a few years back, these were considered bayfront—certainly not the gulf view property you see today!"

Historical maps confirm that this part of Dog Island is eroding especially quickly. The bayshore is losing about one meter of sediment every year, and, at the same time, the Gulf beach steadily loses sand. During the last twenty-five years, the middle of the bone-shaped island has been washing away at about seven feet each year. As the island thins in width, much of its sand is redeposited on the island's eastern and western tips. Viewed on a map, the island reminds me of an embryo lying on its back, slowly unfolding the curl from its neck and legs.

MY SON DAVID was two years old the first time he pulled the smooth wooden handle on Tallahassee's Museum of Florida History's most enduring exhibit. His head barely topped the flat display case that depicts Florida as it existed twelve thousand years ago, when its landmass was roughly twice as large as it is today. As David's hand drew the knob down, a thick indigo liquid compressed our peninsula—and the sea level—into the present day. Every child loves the responsive quality of this exhibit. Over and over, in and out, you can cause the Gulf to retreat and rise, retreat and rise, just as it has, countless times, over the past 2 million years. Just as the human race is causing it to do today—by warming the atmosphere, melting the planet's ice, and raising the level of the sea.

Perhaps it would be helpful if the museum would add another dimension to the interactive exhibit that so charmed my child, an additional slot for the knob that would bring the bright blue Gulf to its inevitable destination fifty years from now, or one hundred, drowning Eastpoint and Carrabelle, St. Teresa and San Blas, and all the islands. Would we still believe we can draw fixed lines—and roads and buildings—on a landscape of unstable sand? Would we still build vacation homes where we construct them today?

"DOG ISLAND could be gone in one day," said Chris Teaf, chairman of the island's conservation district board. "You should approach it like you would any gambling venture. If you can't afford to lose, you shouldn't bet."

Jeff and I had invited Chris to join us for lunch at a small Greek café near Florida State University where both men teach. Chris, too, loved Dog. I wanted to know why he thinks people buy or construct new houses directly in the path of sea-level rise and storm. We knew he had built one himself.

"Dog Island intrigued me," Chris told us. "After I spent one weekend out there at the Pelican Inn, I never looked at any other place." Chris spoke in measured tones, like the scientist he was. His colorful, carefully pressed shirt reflected his passion. "Redfish, bluefish, mackerel, whatever is running out there—that's the draw for me," he said.

"Dog Island has a self-selected population," Chris continued. "People want to live there for the same reasons that make it so hard to visit. It's remote. There's no ferry or bridge. You can only get there by private boat, charter, or small aircraft."

Few of the houses on Dog are the made-for-profit rental palaces that crowd the shores of neighboring St. George Island, and you don't hear talk of beach renourishment or giant riprap brought in from faraway quarries as you do at Alligator Point and Cape San Blas. Even as the island wriggles out from under the foundations of houses and tumbles them into the sea, Dog Island homeowners seem unusually accepting of the inevitable movement of the sand.

Perhaps that's partly due to the creed laid down by Jeff Lewis, a member of a prominent Tallahassee banking family, when he purchased the island after World War II. Some longtime Dog Island residents appreciatively call Lewis their "benevolent dictator," controlling as he did the development of the island between the 1950s and the 1980s. In 1981 the Nature Conservancy acquired Lewis's unsold parcels and now protects three-quarters of the island's eighteen hundred acres in a wilderness area that bears his name. Only twenty people actually live on the island year-round; the others come and go, part time.

"Not everyone who owns property on Dog Island is a committed conservationist, not by far," said Chris. "But the homeowners—about 125 of them—love the benefits of the Nature Conservancy's ethos—a solitary landscape sculpted only by natural forces." That's a good thing, because dozens of houses have been bulldozed by storm surges and full-blown hurricanes. Homeowners either rebuild farther back or just let it go and move inland.

"Dog Islanders are as emotionally connected to their bit of the coast as anyone else," said Chris. "Most people out there have been quite successful in life and have spent a lot of time telling other people what to do. Now, many of them want to be left alone."

Chris believed that his would be one of the last houses to succumb to the sea. "We chose an interior lot four hundred feet back from the water, and we built to Dade County Category 5 hurricane standards on pilings thirty-two feet in the ground, probably unnecessarily deep.

"But we also built our house with a clear understanding that it could someday be gone," Chris continued. "I don't see how people could imagine otherwise, if they thought about what a barrier island does, how it moves and changes."

AN ENORMOUS BANK of violet thunderclouds rose in the east. The sun was a huge bubble of red, sliding into the level sea. Rosi captured it on her camera. She photographed the rising moon, whiskery hermit crabs, stingrays flicking in the shallows. She seemed especially intrigued by plants that trap sand with their roots on the beach.

"You really like that beach vegetation, don't you?" I asked, watching her hunker on her knees to get just the right shot of a sea oat clump.

"Absolutely," she replied. "After Hurricane Dennis took out our primary dune in 2005, I planted hundreds of sea oats and yuccas here, whatever I could get to grow in front of the house.

"My observation is: when the big waves come in a storm like Dennis, it doesn't matter what kind of artificial armoring or protection you've got. When we first moved out here, there were big discussions on the island about trapping sand with various kinds of man-made structures. I was all for it, and I was so mad at my neighbors because they disagreed. Now I've come to see it as folly because I now understand that walls and groins actually intensify the process of erosion. The natural plants and the dunes they hold in place are probably our best line of defense."

Rosanne described the aftermath of Hurricane Dennis: "That storm brought this island to its knees. I had never seen so much debris in my life—steel beams carried across the island, seven homes crushed and forty-two others left in imminent danger of destruction. Our truck and nearly everyone else's was destroyed, and our front dune was cut away like soft butter with a knife. It was after Hurricane Dennis that I really understood: there is nothing we humans can do to change the course of the sea, except to move ourselves back from the tide line.

"Living on Dog Island teaches me to live in the moment, and yet I can see how very attached I am to watching the pelicans and dolphins and enjoying the beauty with my family." She wrestled again, in her mind, with having built a home on the sand. A shimmer of tears started up in her eyes.

"You do it," she said. "You know you are doing it. You know you're a fool! You know the quest for permanence is leading you astray. But I have learned this about myself—I didn't come to Dog Island for an investment. I'm going to live in and love this place for as long as it's here."

CHAPTER 21

The Edge

THE FIRST RAIN BANDS from Hurricane Dennis lashed the
Florida Keys four hundred miles to the south. In Tallahassee we
had moved our cars out from underneath the weak-limbed sweet
gums, secured the chickens, and firmly tied the tomatoes and
peppers so their stems could withstand the heavy rains to come.
We had dragged our kayaks under the deck, stowed away outdoor
furniture, and filled gas cans for our generator.

Earlier in the day, I had driven down to the state park on St.
George Island to meet the gale as it entered the mouth of the Gulf.
The hazy edge of the storm, harbinger of the next day's fury, was
beginning to unroll from the south to the north. Soon it would
blanket the whole of the Gulf of Mexico and settle on a landfall
target. The air was extraordinarily hot, in the high nineties, and
there wasn't a breath of a breeze. Even the seeds of the sea oats
hung still. It felt as if everything in the natural world were listening and feeling, pulling deep into physical sensation, attending to
the hurricane still hundreds of miles to the south, but spinning
inexorably in our direction.

I sat in the warm salty water up to my neck, rocking in the mel-
low surf. Schools of striped little fishes swam around my body
as if I were an artificial reef, a bulkhead of safety. A black skimmer sliced the interface between sand and sea, its bill startlingly
orange, its back and wings ebony. The bird snapped a small fish
from the shallows and maneuvered it for five or ten seconds into a
head-down position to swallow. Out near the first bar, I could see
thrashing schools of silvery fish. Terns and gulls hurtled after the
baitfish the big ones must have been chasing.

It was good to sit with the still waters as the storm blew into
the Gulf and imagine a time before technology, when the senses

of the body and the movements of the creatures were all you had to predict the impending storms. Native peoples mostly retreated from the coast in summer, because by the time they knew for sure how bad the beating would be, there would be no time, no way, to travel far enough inland to be safe. When I left the island and drove back over the bridge to the mainland, Apalachicola Bay lay flat as a pane of glass, with only the tiniest sheen of ripples.

THERE WAS ALWAYS an edge to the Gulf, a threshold where salt water met with and lapped against the land. But that margin fluctuated uncountable times over the past 35 million years, receding and advancing as the planetary sea level rose and fell. No single one of these coastlines defines Florida once and for all. Where the sea level happened to stand at any one point has no relevance in a geologic time frame.

Earth's stable climate, twelve thousand years of tranquility, is drawing to a close because of the waste products of our industry. The reliable character of the natural world no longer is. Surprisingly swift changes in climate bode especially ill for the hundreds of millions of people and animals around the world who live on the coastal margins. The sea is backing up the coastal plain, simply responding to our human actions. As I write these stories about the North Florida islands, the shore where I grew up has been ravaged by super storm Sandy, and the West endures floods, droughts, and wildfires.

Still, this current profile of islands and shorelines is the only one we have ever known. So to us, it matters.

Even more, it matters to the wild creatures that can live only there. On a winter's shorebird survey in February, I ventured far out on a feathery tip of Lanark Reef, facing Dog Island and the roaming waters of the greater Gulf. I watched a pair of oystercatchers with last year's chick, lonely and a little apart. Big and black cloaked and startle eyed, they belonged to this wild place, and they will stand against the wind and the rising tide, safe, until they are not.

The oystercatchers remind me that we also live at the edge—the end—of a poignant time on this planet, at the termination of the Cenozoic era, the time of the Earth's maximum flowering and biodiversity. We humans have induced a crisis of extinction not just in Florida, not just at the coast, but all over this planet. So much more than our geography will be lost as sea level rises. With a conservative one-meter rise in sea level by the year 2100, 98 percent of nesting habitat (sandy beaches) currently used by loggerhead sea turtles along our coast will be lost. Imperiled shorebirds like snowy plovers that also nest only on beaches will be profoundly affected. They are projected to lose more than 90 percent of the habitat they currently occupy.

Planetwide, writes Elizabeth Kolbert in her 2014 book, *The Sixth Extinction*, "one third of all reef-building corals, a third of all freshwater mollusks, a third of sharks and rays, a quarter of all mammals, a fifth of all reptiles, and a sixth of all birds are headed toward oblivion." It's almost unimaginable, yet probable, that the sea turtles and snowy plovers that we share our beaches with (as well as the islands themselves) may not survive this century.

THE END is different from the edge. All life on Earth is not going away. But how much is lost, and how quickly, depends on whether we begin to accommodate other, more ancient claims. We have no right to stay ignorant and continue on, oblivious.

As long as humans inhabited this coast, I am certain there was always someone squatting, sitting, or walking, paying close attention to the edge. Someone who saw new sand bars emerging, and the nuptials of the herons, and the north and south passages of migratory birds. Someone who saw the European sails come tracking over the horizon, and the first signs of hurricanes. Contemporary artist Theodore Morris has created pictorial renderings of Florida's vanished tribes, people who have been forgotten over the centuries. But when you look into their eyes, you can tell that they were watchers at the edge. In their expressions you can see their grave concern as the world they knew collapsed. We are not the first.

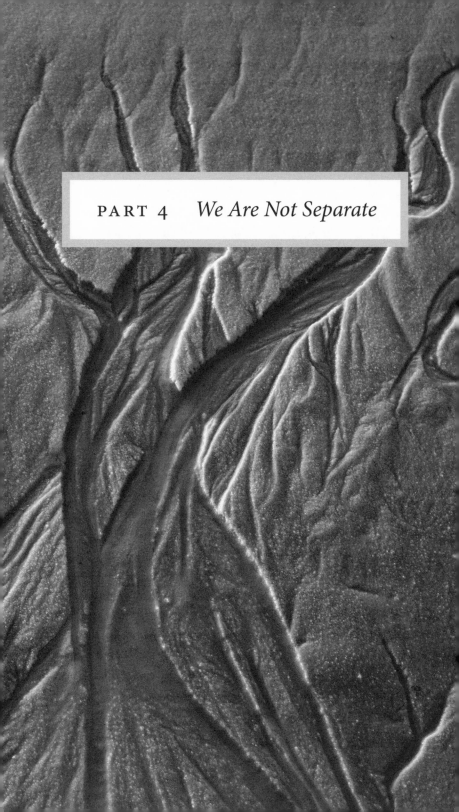

PART 4   *We Are Not Separate*

Human enterprise is scalding Earth's oceans and atmosphere, and ripping apart the fabric of life. What keeps us from stopping those destructive practices is how we have been taught to distance ourselves from the pain of the world.

Know that it is possible to dissolve that separation between ourselves—the human species—and the rest of life on Earth. To be part of the healing, this is the first step we must take. We can retrieve what might it look and feel like to live in synchrony and balance with our places. More than our own desires, we must long for and love the life of the Earth and the unborn of all species waiting for their chance at glorious life.

CHAPTER 22

Candlemas   *Reclaiming the Rhythm of Time*

ONE YEAR, we rented a house at Indian Pass starting on the second day of February—Candlemas—the halfway point between the winter solstice and the spring equinox. I wanted to watch the increase in daylight that had commenced just before Christmas, and how the days would rush and lengthen, and the long nights shrivel at their selvages. I wanted to live inside the cycles of this coast, from one full moon to the next. I wanted to feel the sweep of winter's last fronts coming across the continent. I wanted to pay attention to the wind, how it clocked around the compass and brought rains curtaining in from the west. I wanted to fall asleep to the beating of those spring storms, knowing that when I awoke, new birds would be standing on the beach. A month's sabbatical: I understood my privilege.

THE FIRST MORNING, I stepped onto the porch with my binoculars looped over my neck and a red blanket wound around my shoulders. The sky was still gray, like feathers. A bitter wind glazed my cheeks and teared up my eyes.

Beyond the confines of the house, I entered a vast room of living.

Down at the boat ramp, I watched oystermen launch their square-sterned boats and grind toward Pickalene Bar. Several dozen sea ducks trembled over my head, aiming at the deep Gulf. Three hooded mergansers floated the tide past the porch.

I walked east, watching an apricot glow pool behind the island's pines. A forested chalice was preparing for the sun. The glow became a spreading, molten magma—then, a rosy mounting hill. I startled when the sun crowned the horizon. I had to remind myself it is not that orb that ascends, but our wide planet that rolls toward its star. There was nothing in my sensory receptors that would lead me to this conclusion.

Other animals responded to the gathering energy of the dawn. Dolphins came huffing down the tide from the ramp. They herded fish with their bodies and shoved small waves against the shore. Two of the dolphins paused, lifted from the water and faced the first light. Their chests and heads stained pink. I believed that, like me, they rose to see the sun. Small yellow-rumped warblers and a single mockingbird struck up calling in the dunes. Wind-up sanderlings and willets resumed where they left off the previous evening, foraging in the foam that crumpled along the water's edge. If you live on a round planet that spins on her axis, then you, like every other living thing, must attune to her turning.

The sun sailed. It was just one moment, and now I was in another.

MY INTENTION for the month was to feel my own fit into the ancient cycles of the planet, as humans once did. In town we lived in comfortably conditioned spaces, and we traveled about in cars cooled and heated at great expense to the balance of carbon in the atmosphere. We excluded ourselves from insects and humidity, yes, but also from the great outer world. Too often, I found myself disconnected from the rhythms of the Earth. So I did not know when to expect the tides, nor the exact time of sunrise and sunset, not even the phase of the moon, although I could look every bit of this up. This Candlemas month, we would expose ourselves more fully to the true demands of the elemental planet, and move among its secrets.

GREAT BLUE HERONS must dance to maintain their marriage. If I held perfectly still, they allowed me to watch the renewal of their vows. But I could not move, not even to lift my binoculars from my chest, once the ritual began. That much respect was required.

Over the preceding months, the herons had grown lacy aigrettes (breeding plumes), like purple prayer shawls, to signal their readiness to breed. Side by side, in perfect synchrony, they stepped to the water, and as they processed, they arched their ornamental wings, trailing the very tips into the water. They stood knee-deep, their bills pointing to the sky. They turned as one and strode back up the beach. Again, they pivoted, and suddenly, the dance was done. The cords that ritually bound them relaxed. Both herons stared across the water, orienting to the island where they had built a nest in a tall pine. Or maybe, like me, to the flare of the sun. Or perhaps to the water, looking for small fish to fill their stomachs.

A cold blast of north wind ruffled the feathers of the closer heron into a gossamer scarf around its neck. The tall bird eyed me as I scrambled to my feet. Might I be a source of a fish? Hunger and the habit of begging from anglers drove the great blue to step my way. I watched how the bird articulated its toes and lifted them just high enough to curl closed, as a human might form a fist. One toe drooped, dragging a line in the sand. Between us lay a perfect pink shrimp at the wrack line, someone's left-behind bait. Snap went the beak. Breakfast.

THE SALTWATER TIDES rush up and flood, then fall and withdraw, in a rhythm more permanent than any human construct, two low tides and two high in every twenty-four-hour stretch. But Indian Pass obeyed only itself. Its patterns were mysterious. None of the charts for nearby waters—the Apalachicola River mouth, West Pass, Port St. Joe—reliably predicted their ascent and fall.

When I wanted to cross over the pass, I studied the currents before I stepped into my boat, looking for a slack tendril along one shore or the other that I could use to my advantage. Often an asynchronous ribbon of water pushed in while the rest throbbed gulfward, especially when the tide was paid out fast by a new or full moon. It was worth the time it took to find it.

Over the years I had clipped and pasted the tidal charts that corresponded to our visits into my journals, paired with frustrated notes about what really happened in the pass. Apalachicola Bay straddles a transitional region between the diurnal (one high tide each day) tides of West Florida and the semidiurnal (two high tides each day) rhythms of the Florida peninsula. To complicate matters even further, tides on this Northwest Florida coast are much affected by the wind; during periods of prolonged gusting, the astronomic tide may be completely obscured. Strong southeast or northeast winds markedly increase the flow in both Indian and West Passes.

One summer Jeff and I pounded plastic pipes into the sand at the high- and low-water marks. About twenty feet from shore, we secured a round mushroom anchor with a Styrofoam float attached. Then we could observe the inlet's pulse as it sluiced the float out to sea or sucked it back up the lagoon. At any moment we could line up the three points visually and answer the question, "Is the tide coming in or is it going out?" It was important to know, and not just because the tides form one of the great cycles that hold us and everything else that lives here. It was also very practical. We floated, fished, and moved about almost at will in the pass on days with only two tides, because the waters were not moving as much.

The key to understanding how the tides work is to envision the relationship between the motion of our planet and its moon. The gravitational pull of the moon and the spinning of Earth on its axis cause water to circle the Gulf's great basin, as if a miner settled gold into a pan. Around full and new moon, the powerful alignment of sun and moon and Earth swell the saltwater Gulf to its very brim. All life responds. In the salt marshes littorina snails must hump higher than usual up the stalks of cordgrass to escape their predators, and the little crabs must plug their burrows. Water birds move into the tall marshes and blue crabs swim and scuttle sideways farther upriver than you would imagine, well past the interface of salt water and fresh.

The lowest tides are all seaward and urgent, as if a giant turkey baster sucked the river out to sea. Since the moon has such power over the waters of the planet, wouldn't we wonder how it affects our own liquid bodies? I no longer experience monthly tides of fertility. Still, as an animal, I must be imprinted with other true measures of time, with rhythms so powerful that I ought to be able to live from my inborn, inarguable, genetically gifted connection to the Earth. Even sleep: I noticed that when the bedroom at the coast was lit by moonglow, I woke frequently in the night. Around the new moon, my sleep was deeper, and my days more energetic.

AT INDIAN PASS, the sun was the chief clock of our sabbatical days, but we also watched the moon. Her slim smile followed the track laid out by the sun, across the sky. In full dark, the moon's crescent was a lamp, lighting the whole of her face. The crescent moon meant we had one half-cycle—fourteen days—left of our stay, from that new moon to the full. When I woke at night, there was a canopy over my head: the stars, the stars, the stars.

A tremendous cold front lashed the upper Gulf of Mexico. As it pounded across the continent, it shook down sleet and snow. It drove a torrent of rain over the pass, muffling the day from the sun. Outside my window, terns and gulls continued to fish, but the bald eagles could not or would not fly. The weather kept us grounded as well. Instead of adventuring, I watched the storm, an enormous blue-gray animal, as it rolled from the west to the east.

On the heels of the rain, an Arctic-born wind came raging. The outer Gulf roiled with unusual surf. By the next morning, the storm had forced a crowded mix of at least ten species of shorebirds to the relative protection of the beach below our deck. I carried my tea to the window to watch. The mood of the flock was irritable. Ruddy turnstones, which I think of as sweet-tempered, clownish little birds, snapped at one another and flushed their own kind from the limited space. Three or four black-bellied plovers, tall and thick bodied, shifted from one foot to the other in the midst of the group. Usually they forage singly, off to the edges of feeding flocks. Their tendency to solitude must have been overridden by the need for a space out of the wind. In the middle of the flock, a short-billed dowitcher hunkered against the sand, conserving what warmth it could. The plovers and the dowitcher were birds I hadn't seen yet that week. They had been blown to the beach by the western winds, creatures of weather, unpredictable and awesome. Long slanting rays of sun broke through the cloud fleece over the island. The birds chattered in their unusual abundance, and I felt so grateful to watch.

Another cold front shortstopped a rare avocet and a long-billed curlew on our beach. One morning I found that one hundred weary dunlin had landed in the night. They stood on one leg and did not flush, even though I was so close to them on our porch.

For thousands of years, people kept time by the gathering of the fish and the changing presence of the birds. Among the cast of characters that animated the pass in February were pods of red-breasted mergansers, each topped with a thin, spiky mohawk of feathers. They spoke among themselves in tinny voices. Their calls sounded like hard rain bouncing off a roof in an uneven pattern. The determined cut of their bills precisely aligned with one another as they swam in formation, up or down the tide. When they spied a school of small fish, they snaked in and out of the water. Where I had just counted twenty-three mergansers, momentarily there were only two. Another winter bird, the Bonaparte's gull, benefited from the work of the mergansers. Tiny and raucous, these gulls-in-miniature lifted ahead of the mergansers, trying to snag the fishes they caught. As I watched those winter birds navigate the pass, I thought about how they would soon depart along currents of air, not water, to their northern breeding grounds. We would not see them in the summer.

BY THE END of the month, the moon approached full, so bright that even at midnight I could see the pearly beach, the pass, and the long, low hump of trees on the island. When I arose from my bed and walked outside to look at the sky, I could detect only the skeletons of the constellations. Orion, Cassiopeia, the Pleiades, bleached thin by the moon, were strung together by only the very brightest of their stars, placeholders to remind me that at new moon, the sky would again be honeycombed with light.

DURING THAT long slow Candlemas month, I remembered that my body is always present on the Earth. It is my mind that goes somewhere else. With a gift of time to engage with the living edge of the continent, I spent many, many hours abiding within my life, feeling its rub against my heart. But soon our sabbatical would end. We would pack the truck and drive back to our home in town, to the garden and friends that sustain us, and to our daily tasks in the world. I would leave the pass so sadly, feeling as if I were saying goodbye to the world.

CHAPTER 23

Red Wolves

AT FOUR O'CLOCK in the morning, a long drawn howl drifted
over the water and insinuated my dream. I was sleeping, but the
red wolf was not. Maybe she stalked a raccoon or rodent, teaching her pup to hunt. Perhaps they had filled their bellies and with
dawn approaching, she wished to relocate her mate on the island.
Contact, she requested. Reunion.

I went out to the front beach after sunrise and kneeled beside
a double row of fresh tracks with tight toe prints. A red wolf had
loped along the sand beyond the reach of the waves. She had a
long stride and large feet. Her pup's tracks were precise and delicate, the size of a silver dollar. I continued walking the path of
the wolves along the wrack line. They had stepped over the same
downed logs as I did now, dodged the same drowned pines. A
wild hog had also left a trail of hoof prints, and in the sand I could
read the story of its wanderings from one point of interest to the
next—from the shell of a horseshoe crab to a rubber oysterman's
glove to a ghost crab's burrow. This last must have seemed most
promising, for the pig had excavated it into a crater. When the
wolves' sign veered up into the dunes, I followed. The sand had
been pressed all over with paw prints. I chose a spot to sit where
I wouldn't mar them, wanting to feel the recent presence of these
profoundly endangered canids. But ghost crabs had already scur-
ried their looping script over the places where the wolves had so
recently walked.

Once, I saw an adult red wolf flicker across a sand road at the
eastern end of the island. I stopped and squatted, and the wolf did,
too. She paused on her haunches like a dog, scratched her neck
with one back paw. Her body language was relaxed and showed
no indication of threat. She wore a collar around her neck, a

transmitter that emitted pulse signals biologists could read with a radio receiver to locate her. This wolf was accustomed to human contact. She was part of an effort that since 1990 has managed a small pack—a family—of endangered red wolves on St. Vincent National Wildlife Refuge. Pups born and raised here are relocated into the wild at the Alligator River National Wildlife Refuge in coastal North Carolina.

THE WOLF and the panther have been assigned far more than their share of our overcivilized culture's fear. For love of the night, for wide-ranging territories, for their roles as predators, for these things they have been hunted within a razor's edge of extinction.

One of my father's great gifts to me was to love the dark and its creatures. But there was a time when the rumor of a mountain lion terrified all the parents in our small town in northern New Jersey, including my dad. Only patches and bits of forest remained in Berkeley Heights—not enough to permit the thriving of long-tailed, wide-ranging pumas. But the spine of rocky woodland that divided our home on Sutton Drive from Mountain Avenue to the north might have offered a temporary trail for a big cat searching for a truer habitat.

During the scare, our mother pulled in the boundaries of our outdoor play, back from the rock wall that demarcated our property from the commonly held forest, to the grassy lawn. My father dug out his army revolver from a steel barrel in our attic, where he kept the khaki duffels and other gear from his stint in the Second World War. The black weapon in my father's hand frightened me more than the possibility of a wildcat. No one I knew ever saw that panther, but the thought that it might have passed near us, stepping along our mountain ridge, thrilled me.

The few wolves on St. Vincent Island aren't truly wild, but their instincts are, and I sense that in their voices. The female's howl is not directed at me, but if I happen to be in her matrix, the sound-scape we share, the wolf's voice rouses me. Our culture has taught us to be afraid of wild animals, and to subdue the natural world. In so doing, we also tamp down our own instinctual selves. We must open to the experience of living in the community of nature—being a part of it, not separate from it, certainly not above it.

All human children are born with senses and souls tuned to the cycles of the great turning Earth. Too often they are taken from us. Here is how it happened to me. In grade school, my teachers began to instruct me to stay within the lines. I was contained behind a wooden desk fastened to the floor, expected to remain in my chair. I was bored, but I understood my choices. Live between the lines of penmanship, math, spelling, and reading, or stare out the window at the sky. Reading was the only place my mind had the possibility to fly. There were no birds in the classrooms, just rows of cooped-up children in training to be adults. We were shaped into grown-ups who did not question working from nine to five inside buildings, with unstructured outside time limited to weekends and brief vacations.

Even as good as I was, I rarely earned straight A's, although my sister did. I believe I lost heart in the rote tasks. In a note to my parents, the teacher offered a clue as to how to achieve more perfect progress reports.

She wrote, "Sue doesn't always pay attention in class. She's too dreamy."

So at the start of the new grading period, I began to stare at the teacher with all my focus, with the intensity I had reserved for the clouds, or the stories in my books at home. The teacher finally said, "Is everything all right? Is something the matter with you, Sue?" She was uncomfortable with the fixed gaze I thought would bring me solid A's, the cultural yardstick of success for a young schoolchild. My focus did not equal true engagement. If I had been paying attention to my own indigenous mind, I would have revolted from the system that was training me.

The wild birds tried to help me. In penmanship lessons, they slipped between the lines. The capital S of my name transformed into a mother duck, after I sketched in an eye and a small beak. I played with the forward lean of the letter. Now the duck promised movement even as she swam over the straight furrows inscribed on the paper. She paddled as fast as she could between those lines, two straight and one dashed—and right behind her came a row of lowercase s's. Again with the addition of an eye and small triangular bills, they became ducklings, rows and rows of ducklings trying to swim from between the prison bars of the paper. I longed to follow them off the page and out the window to the sky and lakes beyond.

AT THE END of each school day, I returned to our backyard. It was a small world, just a remnant stand of old trees, but the shade they offered was complete. There was a flat stump we children called our throne and an area of raised, gnarly roots we converted into a commissary of acorns, tulip tree daggers, berries, maple seeds, and mushrooms. There were lightning bugs in the summer evenings and deep snow drifts in January. We didn't have to go far to travel deep into tree-sponsored play. Grown-ups never entered our imaginative place. It offered me a whiff of the wild.

In 1960, when I was in the third grade, the Great Dismal National Wildlife Refuge was established less than six miles from my home. It protected twelve square miles of New Jersey forest and wetland wilderness. My father read to us from the local newspaper about the swamp's protection. He described it as a place of significance and interest, one we should certainly visit. The refuge bird list contains the soundscape of the whole of my adult life. If we had visited there when I was a young person, I might have seen every wild duck I learned to identify later on in my twenties, and every wood warbler, too. But our family explorations were held in check by the weight and clamor of four children under the age of seven, and so we never did go.

The Earth insinuates herself into all living things, is all living things, so it's no wonder that although I never saw the golden prothonotary warblers breeding in the Great Swamp, when I did meet them with my own eyes in the forested wetlands of the southeastern United States, my joy was so great. Since we had been separated by suburban life and my own ignorance, since I had no one who knew their names and habits, nor led me to them, no wonder my delight at our first physical encounter. I had traveled and studied and breathed on this continent during the early decades of my life, isolated from the wild warbler and the beauty of the bunting and the long-billed curlew. I was disconnected from the birds and my own wild nature by a lack of proper schooling. I simply did not know.

But the Earth has been reclaiming me all of my life, enticing my eyes out the windows, offering yet one more chance, and then another, and then another, to be enfolded in her original mind. This is the good news of our mutual resilience. The Earth can still infuse us.

Even now, I spot the movement of true birds when I am behind plate glass windows. My eyes lock onto swirls of cedar waxwings in early May outside the second-story window of the gym. I know when I go back outside exactly where to look for them, mobbing the berries of the holly trees. When I pass by a park, I don't miss the red-shouldered hawk standing on St. Augustine grass under tall pines. She knows I am watching her, too. Through the windshield of my car, I also see bald eagles and kites—both Mississippi and swallow-tailed—in their seasons.

Why are we kept inside? Why do we allow ourselves to remain there? I count the days of the year that I can sleep out of doors, call it a good twelve months if I bedded in a tent or on a sailboat two or three weeks out of fifty-two. The wild Earth waits for me there.

CHAPTER 24

We Are Not Separate

I CROUCHED on a stair step close to the beach, blending in as best I could, so I wouldn't disturb the wild birds. Wind puffed against my neck. Small waves shushed over the sand. I watched one of the resident great blue herons snag a needlefish from the surf, pound it limp, rinse it in the salt water, then flip it around to swallow, head first and needle down.

The heron retreated to digest its meal on the largest limb of the pine tree that shaded me. I willed myself to be as still as the steps so I wouldn't scare it away. Shifting his weight to one leg, the bird began the task of maintaining his feathers. He dug deep into the down, nibbling each quill free of cuticle. He closed the membranes over his eyeballs to protect their glisten from grit. The repetitive motions of grooming lulled the bird into sleepiness. As I watched, the heron shrunk his neck down into its body and gave in to sleep. His shuttered eye was colored the same gray blue as the bill. The design of the great blue heron's head, I noted, was all one weapon—eye to bill to neck—all one efficient tool for fishing.

Other people trickled out from their rental cottages to be on the beach, including our neighbors on the left, a sunburned young father and Caitlin, his daughter. Caitlin had the look of a girl who spent a lot of hours alone with her outdoorsman dad. Any wind could tangle her hair, unbound by a mother's careful braids or pigtails. She was a child who could entertain herself while her father baited his hooks and cast them into the current. She was long legged and knob kneed and always on the move, singing and talking to herself and her father and the fish in her father's bucket. She was curious, and in conversation with all of the living expressions of the pass.

And she was alert to the wild birds. I saw that about her right away. The eagle that caught my eye, she also acknowledged with a swivel of her head, following its flight over to the island. When a second great blue heron began her dance down near the boat ramp, enticing her mate in my tree, Caitlin's own limbs took note and followed, copying the angular lift of the bird's knee and wing. Her arms opened like the heron's two lacy parasols: unscripted, unconscious, loose jointed, girl joyous. The wind took her hair, just as it lifted the bird's glimmery plumes. I deeply admired her physical communion with all that was. She was the closest thing to crossing over to being bird that I'd ever seen.

She was the answer to this question: how did we stop seeing ourselves as deeply embedded participants in the cycles of the planet? Here was her answer: some of us still are. All of us can be.

Down along the shore, another fisherman set up his poles and his baits. I heard a rustle of wings over my head. My great blue heron, hoping for a handout, left the tree and took up a post about fifty yards behind the man. His stance was as taut as the angler's line, tugged hard by the tide.

"Look, look!" someone yelled from the shore. A dolphin arced through the air and smacked down hard, leaving a smoothed pool on the surface of the water. All the little wavelets were quieted by the dolphin's blow. I heard its forceful exhale. Two, three, four, five more times it leaped toward the sky. Sunlight poured through cracks between the platinum clouds. Everybody and everything along the shore seemed alive and ecstatic.

Meanwhile, the angler had hooked a catfish. He tossed the spiny creature to the waiting heron, and the bird began a brisk stalk to claim it. From the high pines above the dunes, a bald eagle swooped down and drove the heron off the catfish, taking it for his own. The bird squawked, severely disappointed. My heart shimmied in my rib cage.

THESE are the moments when we remember that Earth is sacred—when we see the leap of the dolphin, the scramble of the turtle over the beach, the blaze of a shooting star. These are opportunities Earth gives us to open wide our minds. We are invited to say, Ahhhh! We are taken quite outside of ourselves. Our consciousness enlarges and becomes permeable. Our steps slow, and our thoughts relax. These are the moments when we are reminded that we are the universe, in the form of the Earth, in the form of a human, at this time and place on the planet.

Despite our pirating of the atmosphere, the land, the waters, and the wildlife, Earth still speaks to us and shares her creations. "What will you do in return," she asks us, "to help this life continue?"

Saint Island Prayer

Align us, o beauteous Earth
with your purposes.

Open our ears, our inner and outer eyes
to the particular work you would have us do
to the work we fit as closely
as the plunging tern, embraced by salt shallows
as the palm deeply rooted in shell mound
as the wind, wrestling through it all
and beyond, the glaring sun.

We are hungry to know what we may do.
We listen and watch
We attend.
Our lives are so short, our hearts, so strong.
We know that in serving your life forms,
We also serve ourselves.

Teach us to be
as persuasive as the pelican
as inevitable as the ancestor
as peaceful as the oyster
as relentless as the raptor
as relaxed as the tide
as reliable as the moon
as present as the palm to the wind.

SUSAN CERULEAN
St. Vincent Island, Florida
November 2004

ACKNOWLEDGMENTS

FOR EVERY POSSIBLE kind of support, I thank my husband, Jeff Chanton. My dream is Jeff's dream, as well: to deeply experience and understand the wild edge of our coast as it is, as it has been, and as it might be in the years to come. An important fiber in our marriage is the fierce joy of living in this very particular time and place on the planet. For me there is no better companion.

During the years I have been writing *Coming to Pass*, my friend David Moynahan has been matching my words with his camera and his exceptional eye for beauty. David's artistry is well known in Florida, and he's got many award-winning endeavors of his own (see www.davidmoynahan.com). Still, every time I'd ask, "David, do you think you could get a great picture of an oystercatcher (or a retreating shoreline or a red wolf)?" he would do it. He would rise before dawn and figure out an angle and a light that would exceed my expectations. All this he gave as a friend and as an advocate for wild Florida. In the spring of 2014 it was a great joy to pore over David's archives with him and select the final images for this book. Thank you from the bottom of my heart, generous friend.

Crystal Wakoa loves the birds as much as I do. Her companionship and wisdom are irreplaceable. I thank multitalented Matt Smith for making beautiful maps, and so quickly.

Poet Mary Jane Ryals met with me every week for an entire year while we wrote and revised our books. Her support and careful reading made my solitary work possible. Poet, activist, intellectual, and kind man Dan Corrie, I owe you big time. Margaret Clark is the best reference librarian I know, and I am ever so grateful for her help and her love. No one cheered me and encouraged me to seek the biggest possible picture more than my dear friend Norine Cardea. Janisse Ray, you are always with me.

Thank you to my precious son, David Canter, for research assistance and for all that you are. My sister Roberta, with an A-line of mysteries, reminded me to stay in my seat and get it done. My family is the best: Don, Roberta, Doug and Martha Isleib, Patrick and Casey Chanton, and all my beloved nieces and nephews, in-laws, and cousins. I am grateful to my parents and all my ancestors who gave me life and a solid footing in an impermanent world. Hannah Kauffman-Skloff and her family are also dear to me. Thank you for your many kindnesses.

No book can live without its champions. Dale Julian, Sandy March, and Buddy the cat tend to the writers of Florida, and make our work possible at Apalachicola's independent Downtown Books. Charlotte Chumney has sustained the U.S. Fish and Wildlife Service's St. Vincent National Wildlife Refuge office in Apalachicola for many decades. She helped me find the memory of the island stored in the refuge files.

I am deeply indebted to the people who allowed me to interview and accompany them in their work on behalf of our coast. Any errors in this book are my own, not theirs. In 2012 Barbara Stedman unexpectedly died of congestive heart failure in Cookeville, Tennessee. Although a record of her work remains, including 174 Christmas Bird Counts, her personally experienced understanding of the birds of the northern Gulf Coast cannot be replaced. I will always be grateful for her mentorship.

I am so grateful to the awesome folks at University of Georgia Press, especially Patrick Allen, Jon Davies, Elizabeth Crowley and the talented art department. Thanks to Sue Breckenridge for meticulous copyediting.

My life and work is always enriched by the circles that hold me: Womenspirit, Heart of the Earth, the dream circle, Velma Frye's singing circle, and most of all, my longtime writing circle, Donna Klein, Velma Frye, and Amrita Brummel-Smith. For helping me keep spirit, body, and home together, I thank Teri and Sami Washburn, Sarah Portillo, Angie Rignanese, Loretta Armer, Ellen Shapiro, and Gretchen Hein.

What great good fortune I had to work on this book during a second residency at Hedgebrook on Whidbey Island. Thank you, visionary women.

John Brady, Tom Clark, Lou Cross, Ian MacDonald, Ann Morrow, Jeff Newberry, Becky Reardon, Wilderness Sarchild, Bradley Smith, Elise Smith, John Spohrer, Dan Tonsmeire, Shannon Lease and all the Apalachicola Riverkeepers, and Barry Fraser and Lucy Ann Walker-Fraser, thank you.

Marlee LeDai, a wonderful teacher and a caring friend, asked all the right questions as I worked on earlier drafts of this book. Check out her classes on writers.com. Deena Metzger urged me to go deep, deep, deeper. Deena's wisdom, and the courage and brilliance of Terry Tempest Williams, Kathleen Dean Moore, Miriam MacGillis, Linda Hogan, Thomas Berry, and Leslie Marmon Silko inspire me always.

NOTES

INTRODUCTION   THE PASSING OF A PALM CATHEDRAL

5   Three-quarters of Florida's population lives in coastal zone: Cerulean
     2008.
10   I calculated the approximate level of greenhouse gases—300 parts
     per million—in our atmosphere during the late 1950s from a graph
     known as the Keeling curve, which tracks CO_2 concentration in
     the troposphere at Mauna Loa, 1950s–present: Schlesinger and
     Bernhardt 2012.

1   SAND SUPPLY

17   "The Summer Day," in Oliver 1990, 60.
17   Sea level: Donoghue and White 1995; Donoghue 2011.
17   How shoreline reached present position, and formation of islands:
     Bush et al. 2001; Pilkey 1990.

2   FRONT BEACH

25   Hundred-year-old monograph describes a St. Vincent Island recog-
     nizable today: Hornaday 1909, 5.

3   RELICT RIDGES

36   Aging of the dune ridges on St. Vincent Island: Forrest 2007; Lopez
     and Rink 2008.
40   Natural history of the sambar deer: Lewis et al. 1990.
44   St. Vincent's forests and how they fell: Hornaday 1909, 5 and 14;
     Johnson 1943; Miller, Griffin, and Fryman 1980.

49 Establishment of late Archaic Indians along coast: Donoghue and White 1995; and Miller, Griffin, and Fryman 1980; White 2008; White 2011.

54 Water filtration rate for scallops: Florida Marine Research Institute 1998.

5 THE PASSES

61 Use of West Pass in early 1800s: Owens 1966.
61 This voluminous journal contains a wealth of terse observations about island life in the late 1800s: Wefing 1879, 83.
64 Wefing 1879, 153.
66 Wefing 1879, 259.
68 Stingray as a pancake version of a shark: Grubbs 2008.

6 UPLAND: WHERE THE BEACH USED TO BE

76 For more on the geological and cultural history of the Buffer Preserve, see *St. Joseph Bay State Buffer Preserve Management Plan* 2012.

7 THE FIRST PEOPLE

87 Important summary of what is known about the Panhandle's prehistoric ancestors: Hann 2006.
88 Shepard 1998, 167.
88 Description of how early villages grew: Milanich 1995.
89 Journal excerpt from 1693 colonizer Gongora and the Pez expedition: Hann 2006; Milanich 1998.
89 Anecdote regarding French shipwreck victim Pierre Viaud: Fabel 1990, 52–60.
90 How people understand themselves to be connected (or not) to a landscape has everything to do with how they care for the land: Cordova 2007.
90 More from the Pez expedition: Hann 2006.
92 Lopez 1992, 9.

93 For hundreds of years, invasions were a way of life in North Florida: Boyd 1999, 54.

93 In his books *1491* and *1493*, historian Charles Mann—with painstaking eloquence—explains what really happened: Mann 2011, 12.

93 Forbes Purchase: Owens 1966, chapter 2.

94 This quote appeared in official English policy regarding its newly acquired territory on the North American continent. Today we have little idea how extensive the fur trade was in Florida: West 1960, 11.

96 The Forbes purchase opened North Florida to the privatization of land: Owens 1966; Rogers and Willis 2004.

96 Island ownership: Rogers and Willis 2004.

8   BEACH BADGES

101 See Parry 2010.

103 Blew 2001, 93.

103 In late 2013, the original prime meridian marker was replaced by a more visible rendition in Tallahassee's new Cascades Park.

103 See Knetsch 2006.

105 See Parry 2010; Kranz 2011.

106 "Geologically unified wedge": Kaufman and Pilkey 1979, 230.

107 See Berry 2006, one of the most important cultural historians of our time.

9   CLAIMING A SPACE ON THE SAND: WILLETS

113 There is a great deal of research about spacing behaviors of shorebirds; Ehrlich 1988, 387, gives a good overview.

10   WHAT THE EAGLE CALLS HOME

118 The bald eagle, our national emblem, is a threatened species. Quite a bit is known about their nesting requirements: Buehler 2000; Florida Fish and Wildlife Conservation Commission 2008.

120 Eagle population recovery: Buehler 2000.

120 Eagle surveys: Smith 2012.

121 Many indigenous tribes honored the bald eagle: Guss 1985, 39; Krech 2009.

141 Excellent history of local fishing practices, especially seine fishery: Roddenberry 2007.

148 Ten percent or less of the shrimp and we eat today is obtained from trawling wild stocks. Aquaculture of shrimp, much of it overseas, is the source of most of the shrimp we eat, and that method of production brings its own environmental problems: Hart 2012.

148 Although shark populations are diminishing worldwide, many anglers still pursue them: Gerardi 2013.

13 OYSTERCATCHERS

155 Caribbean monk seal extinction in Gulf: NOAA 2008.

156 Sprunt 1954, 156.

158 Virginia Woolf is well known for her contributions to American literature, but she also advocated against the devastation of the plumed birds: Woolf 1920, 3; and McIver 2003.

159 See Kale et al. 2003.

159 See Bent 1929, 312.

160 For protection protocols for American oystercatchers: Meyers 2010.

160 Wright 2013.

14 ROBBING THE RIVER

165 See Cerulean 1994.

168 Whether in left behind middens, or handwritten journals, there is plenty of evidence that people have always loved oysters: Hornaday 1909, 5; Marks 2010; and McNeill 2002.

170 Taylor 2013; Apalachicola Bay Oyster Situation Report, 2013.

171 As goes the water in the bay, so go the oysters: NOAA 2008; Alvarez 2013; Sommer 2013.

15 EVOLUTION'S LARGER CONCERNS: BEACH MICE

177 Beach mice data are from U.S. Department of Interior Fish and Wildlife Service 2010; Enge et al. 2002.

187   CBC data from Butcher and Niven 2007.

188   Data from Florida Fish and Wildlife Conservation Commission 2011.

200   Technical data on effects of light pollution on sea turtles:
Witherington and Martin 2003.

206   See Stevens et al. 2013 for medical studies regarding health effects
of nighttime lighting; compelling article on why we need darkness:
Klinkenborg 2008.

216   See McLendon 2013 for interview on effects of oil spill.

221   See Ward et al. 2006 for details of the lighthouse find as well as other
shipwrecks around Dog Island.

225   Personal communication with Dr. Jeffrey Chanton, Florida State
University, 2014.

227   See map at Save the Cape San Blas Lighthouse—Cape San Blas,
Florida, http://capesanblaslight.org/historic-photos.cfm. More info:
Bush et al. 2001; Cape San Blas Lighthouse Board 1875.

229–30   To read more about Cape San Blas, and Stump Hole in particular:
Portman 2009b. Two essential books to read about the issue of
beach renourishment and the rising sea in general: Pilkey and Young
2009; and Dean 1999.

230   See Liles 2012 regarding National Flood Insurance Program.

237   The *Tallahassee Democrat* published an illuminating series on the
effects of sea level rise on Dog Island and Cape San Blas: Portman
2009a, 2009b.

21 THE EDGE

247 For more about future sea level rise impacts on our coastal resources: Freeman et al. 2012.

247 Kolbert 2013, 17–18.

247 See Morris 2004. His well-researched illustrations of Florida's lost tribes recreate their lives and legacy.

22 CANDLEMAS: RECLAIMING THE RHYTHM OF TIME

256 Regarding Apalachicola Bay area tides: Gorsline 1963.

23 RED WOLVES

264 For more on red wolf project, see *St. Vincent National Wildlife Refuge: Draft Comprehensive Conservation Plan and Environmental Assessment* 2012, 44.

Alvarez, Lizette. 2013. "A Fight over Water, and to Save a Way of Life." *New York Times*, June 2.

Apalachicola Bay Oyster Situation Report. 2013. TP-200. Gainesville, Fla.: National Sea Grant College Program (NOAA).

Bent, Arthur Cleveland. 1929. "American Oystercatcher." In *Life Histories of North American Shorebirds*, part 2:309–16. *United States National Museum Bulletin* 146. Washington, D.C.: Smithsonian Institution.

Berry, Thomas. 2006. *Evening Thoughts: Reflecting on Earth as Sacred Community*. San Francisco: Sierra Club Books.

Blew, Mary Clearman. 2001. *All but the Waltz: A Memoir of Five Generations in the Life of a Montana Family*. Norman: University of Oklahoma Press.

Boyd, Mark F. 1999. *Here They Once Stood: The Tragic End of the Apalachee Missions*. Gainesville: University Press of Florida.

Buehler, David A. 2000. "Bald Eagle (*Haliaeetus leucocephalus*)." In *The Birds of North America Online*, edited by A. Poole. Ithaca: Cornell Lab of Ornithology. doi:10.2173/bna.506.

Bush, David M., Norma J. Longo, William Neal, Luciana Esteves, Orrin H. Pilkey, Deborah Pilkey, and Craig Webb. 2001. *Living on the Edge of the Gulf: The West Florida and Alabama Coast*. Durham: Duke University Press.

Butcher, G. S., and D. K. Niven. 2007. "Common Birds in Decline." National Audubon Society. http://stateofthebirds.audubon.org/cbid.

Cape San Blas Lighthouse Board. 1875. Cape San Blas Light. "Historic Light Station Information & Photography: Florida." U.S. Coast Guard. http://www.uscg.mil/history/weblighthouses/lhfl.asp.

Cerulean, Susan. 1994. "Oysters on the Edge: Taking Stock of Apalachicola Bay's Shellfish Industry." *Florida Travel and Life*, October, 13–15.

——— 2008. *Wildlife 2060: What's at Stake for Florida*. Tallahassee: Florida Fish and Wildlife Conservation Commission. http://myfwc .com/media/129053/FWC2060.pdf.

Chanton, Jeffrey P. Personal communication. 2014.

Cordova, V. F. 2007. *How It Is: The Native American Philosophy of V. F. Cordova*. Tucson: University of Arizona Press.

Dean, Cornelia. 1999. *Against the Tide: The Battle for the American Coast*. New York: Columbia University Press.

Donoghue, Joseph F. 2011. "Sea Level History of the Northern Gulf of Mexico Coast and Sea Level Rise Scenarios for the Near Future." *Climatic Change* 107:17–33.

Donoghue, Joseph F., and Nancy Marie White. 1995. "Late Holocene Sea-Level Change and Delta Migration, Apalachicola River Region, Northwest Florida, USA." *Journal of Coastal Research* 11, no. 3: 651–63.

Ehrlich, Paul R. 1988. *The Birder's Handbook: A Field Guide to the Natural History of North American Birds: Including All Species That Regularly Breed North of Mexico*. New York: Simon & Schuster.

Enge, Kevin M., Brian A. Millsap, Terry J. Doonan, Jeffery A. Gore, Nancy J. Douglass, and Gary L. Sprandel. 2002. *Conservation Plans for Biotic Regions in Florida Containing Multiple Rare or Declining Wildlife Taxa*. Technical Report No. 20. Tallahassee: Florida Fish and Wildlife Conservation Commission.

Fabel, Robin F. 1990. *Shipwreck and Adventures of Monsieur Pierre Viaud*. Pensacola: University of West Florida Press. First published 1768 by P. Viaud, France.

Florida Fish and Wildlife Conservation Commission. 2008. *FWC Bald Eagle Management Plan Handbook*.

——. 2011. *Reddish Egret Biological Status Review Report*.

Florida Marine Research Institute. 1998. "Bay Scallops: Underwater Canaries." Florida Department of Environmental Protection. http ://www.marine.usf.edu/pjocean/packets/sp98/scallop_seastats.pdf.

Forrest, Beth M. 2007. "Evolution of the Beach Ridge Strandplain on St. Vincent Island, Florida." PhD diss., Florida State University.

Freeman, Kathleen, Laura Geselbracht, Doria Gordon, Eugene Kelly, and Laila Racevwskiss. 2012. *Understanding Future Sea Level Rise Impacts on Coastal Wetlands in Apalachicola Bay Region of Florida's Gulf Coast*. DEP Agreement No. CM112.

Gerardi, Jerry. 2013. "Right Time for Sharks." *Tallahassee Democrat*, July 5, Sports sec.

Gorsline, D. 1963. "Oceanography of Apalachicola Bay, Florida." In *Essays in Marine Geology in Honor of K. O. Emery, Los Angeles*, edited by

Thomas Clements, Robert E. Stevenson, Dorothy M. Halmos, 69–96. Los Angeles: University of Southern California Press.

Grubbs, R. Dean. 2008. "Sting Rays." June 12, Florida State University Marine Laboratory.

Guss, David M. 1985. *The Language of the Birds: Tales, Texts, & Poems of Interspecies Communication*. San Francisco: North Point Press.

Hann, John H. 2006. *The Native American World Beyond Apalachee: West Florida and the Chattahoochee Valley*. Ripley P. Bullen Series. Gainesville: University Press of Florida.

Hart, Rick A. 2012. *Stock Assessment of Pink Shrimp (Farfantepenaeus duorarum) in the U.S. Gulf of Mexico for 2011*. Galveston, Tex.: NOAA Fisheries/Southeast Fisheries Science Center.

Hornaday, William T. 1909. *A Monograph on St. Vincent's Game Preserve*. Buffalo, N.Y.

Johnson, Malcolm B. 1943. "Loggers Invade Game Paradise to Fell War Timber." *New York Times*, January 17.

Kale, H. W., II, B. Pranty, B. M. Stith, and C. W. Biggs. 2003. "American Oystercatcher." In *Florida's Breeding Bird Atlas: A Collaborative Study of Florida's Birdlife*. http://legacy.myfwc.com/bba/docs/bba_AMOY.pdf.

Kaufman, Wallace, and Orrin H Pilkey. 1979. *The Beaches Are Moving: The Drowning of America's Shoreline*. Garden City, N.Y: Anchor Press.

Klinkenborg, Verlyn. 2008. "Our Vanishing Night." *National Geographic*, November, 106–9.

Knetsch, Joe. 2006. *Faces on the Frontier*. Cocoa: Florida Historical Society Press.

Kolbert, Elizabeth. 2014. *The Sixth Extinction: An Unnatural History*. New York: Henry Holt.

Kranz, Erika. 2011. "Sand for the People: The Continuing Controversy Over Public Access to Florida's Beaches." http://www.beachapedia.org/State_of_the_Beach/Perspectives/Sand_People.

Krech, Shepard. 2009. *Spirits of the Air: Birds and American Indians in the South*. Athens: University of Georgia Press.

Lewis, J. C., L. B. Flynn, R. L. Marchinton, S. M. Shea, and E. M. Marchant. 1990. *Ecology of Sambar Deer on St. Vincent National Wildlife Refuge, Florida*. Bulletin no. 25. Tallahassee, Fla.: Tall Timbers Research Station.

Liles, Jay. 2012. "Don't Make Us Pay for Poor Decisions." *Tallahassee Democrat*, April 8.

Lopez, Barry Holstun. 1992. *The Rediscovery of North America*. New York: Vintage Books.

Lopez, Gloria I., and W. Jack Rink. 2008. "New Quartz Optical Stimulated Luminescence Ages for Beach Ridges on the St. Vincent Island Holocene Strandplain, Florida, United States." *Journal of Coastal Research* 24, no. 1A: 49–62.

Mann, Charles C. 2006. *1491: New Revelations of the Americas before Columbus*. New York: Vintage.

———. 2011. *1493: Uncovering the New World Columbus Created*. New York: Alfred A. Knopf.

Marks, Charles, Jr. 2010. "St. Vincent Island: Then and Now." *Apalachicola Times*, January 14.

McIver, Stuart B. 2003. *Death in the Everglades: The Murder of Guy Bradley, America's First Martyr to Environmentalism*. Gainesville: University Press of Florida.

McLendon, Russell. 2013. "BP's Oiled Animals: Where Are They Now?" *Mother Nature Network*, April 16. http://www.mnn.com/earth-matters /wilderness-resources/blogs/bps-oiled-animals-where-are-they-now.

McNeill, Jimmy. 2002. "Interview with Jimmy McNeill by Dr. Nancy White, Treasure Bay Lodge, Gulf County, Florida." Unpublished.

Meyers, J. Michael. 2010. *Management, Monitoring, and Protection Protocols for American Oystercatchers at Cape Hatteras National Seashore, North Carolina*. U.S. Geological Survey Open-File Report 2009-1262.

Milanich, Jerald T. 1995. *Florida Indians and the Invasion from Europe*. Gainesville: University Press of Florida.

———. 1998. *Florida's Indians from Ancient Times to the Present*. Gainesville: University Press of Florida.

Miller, James J., John W. Griffin, and Mildred L. Fryman. 1980. *Archaeological and Historical Survey of St. Vincent National Wildlife Refuge, Florida*. Cultural Resource Survey, 1978–79, A-5831 (79). U.S. Fish and Wildlife Service.

Morris, Theodore. 2004. *Florida's Lost Tribes*. Gainesville: University Press of Florida.

NOAA. 2008. *Caribbean Monk Seal (Monachus tropicalis)*. NOAA Fisheries Office of Protected Resources.

Oliver, Mary. 1990. *House of Light*. Boston: Beacon Press.

Owens, H. P. 1966. "Apalachicola before 1861." PhD diss., Florida State University.

Parry, Wayne. 2010. "Jersey Shore Wars: Who Owns the Beaches?" *Gloucester Times*, June 20.

Pilkey, Orrin H. 1990. "Barrier Islands: Formed by Fury, They Roam and Fade." *SeaFrontiers*, December, 30–36.

Pilkey, Orrin H, and Rob Young. 2009. *The Rising Sea*. Washington, D.C.: Island Press/Shearwater Books.

Portman, Jennifer. 2009a. "Dog Island: History and Tenacious Owners Anchor Slipping Sands." *Tallahassee Democrat*, June 28.

———. 2009b. "Cape San Blas Saved—for Now." *Tallahassee Democrat*, June 29.

Roddenberry, David. 2007. *Historic Seine Fisheries of Wakulla County and Eastern Franklin County Florida*. 2nd ed. N.p.: David Roddenberry.

Rogers, William Warren, and Lee Willis. 2004. *At the Water's Edge: a Pictorial and Narrative History of Apalachicola and Franklin County*. Tallahassee, Fla.: Sentry Press.

Schlesinger, William H, and Emily S. Bernhardt. 2012. *Biogeochemistry: An Analysis of Global Change*. Amsterdam: Academic Press. Science Direct. http://www.sciencedirect.com/science/book/9780123858740.

Shepard, Paul. 1998. *Coming Home to the Pleistocene*. Washington, D.C: Island Press.

Smith, Bradley. 2012. Personal communication on bald eagle surveys on St. Vincent Island.

Sommer, Eleanor K. 2013. "Reduced Freshwater Inflow to Florida Panhandle to Blame for Oyster Die-off." http://www.earthisland.org /journal/index.php/elist/eListRead/apalachicola_bay_oyster_die-off _hurts_fishermen/.

Sprunt, Alexander, Jr. 1954. *Florida Bird Life*. New York: Coward-McCann and the National Audubon Society.

St. Joseph Bay State Buffer Preserve Management Plan (Draft). 2012. Tallahassee: Florida Department of Environmental Protection.

St. Vincent National Wildlife Refuge: Draft Comprehensive Conservation Plan and Environmental Assessment. 2012. Atlanta: U.S. Department of the Interior Fish and Wildlife Service.

Stevens, R. G., G. C. Brainard, D. E. Blask, S. W. Lockley, and M. E. Motta. 2013. "Adverse Health Effects of Nighttime Lighting: Comments on

American Medical Association Policy Statement." *American Journal of Preventive Medicine* 45:343–46.

Taylor, Joe. 2013. Interview on the effects of oyster die-offs on Apalachicola oystermen. September 9.

U.S. Department of Interior Fish and Wildlife Service. 2010. *St. Andrew Beach Mouse Recovery Plan*. Panama City, Fla. http://www.fws.gov /PanamaCity/resources.

Ward, Cheryl, Mike Lavender, Cynthia M. Bellacero, James Dixon, and Sean Reynolds. 2006. *Apalachee Bay Maritime Research Project Report of Operations*. Tallahassee: Florida State University Department of Anthropology.

Wefing, George Frederick. 1879. Journal. St. Vincent National Wildlife Refuge, Apalachicola, Florida.

West, G. M. 1960. *St. Andrews, Florida*. 3rd ed. Panama City, Fla.: Panama City Publishing Company.

White, Nancy Marie. 2008. *Archaeology for Dummies*. Hoboken, N.J.: Wiley Publishing.

———. 2011. Interview on St. Vincent archaeology. February 17.

Witherington, Blair E., and R. Erik Martin. 2003. *Understanding, Assessing, and Resolving Light-Pollution Problems on Sea Turtle Nesting Beaches*. FMRI Technical Report TR-2. Florida Fish and Wildlife Conservation Commission.

Woolf, Virginia. 1920. "The Plumage Bill." *Woman's Leader*, July 23.

Wright, Beth. 2013. Personal communication on status of Apalachicola Bay nesting American oystercatchers.